Uncle John's

BEST OF

BRIEFS

TRIVIA YOU CAN
TAKE ANYWHERE

Bathroom Readers'
Institute

Portable Press
San Diego, California

Portable Press
An imprint of Printers Row Publishing Group
10350 Barnes Canyon Road, Suite 100, San Diego, CA 92121
www.portablepress.com • mail@portablepress.com

Publisher: Peter Norton • Associate Publisher: Ana Parker
Publishing/Editorial Team: April Farr, Vicki Jaeger, Kelly Larsen, Tanya Fijalkowski,
Kathryn C. Dalby, Lauren Taniguchi
Production Team: Jonathan Lopes, Rusty von Dyl
Cover design: Rosemary Rae, Rusty von Dyl

The Library of Congress has cataloged the original edition of this title as follows:
Names: Bathroom Readers' Institute
Title: Uncle John's new & improved briefs / Bathroom Readers' Institute.
Description: San Diego, CA : Portable Press, 2018.
Identifiers: LCCN 2018014067 (print) | LCCN 2018022445 (ebook) | ISBN
9781684124183 (ebook) | ISBN 9781684124176 (paperback)
Subjects: LCSH: American wit and humor. | Curiosities and wonders. | BISAC:
REFERENCE / Trivia. | HUMOR/Form/Trivia. | HUMOR/Form/Puns & Wordplay.
Classification: LCC PN6165 (ebook) | LCC PN6165 .U53754 2018 (print) | DDC
818/.602--dc23
LC record available at https://lccn.loc.gov/2018014067

ISBN: 978-1-64517-129-4

Printed in China

23 22 21 20 19   1 2 3 4 5

OUR "REGULAR" READERS RAVE!

"Love your books and have quoted them often. Thanks for the fun, informative reads!"

—**Bob**

"Your books bring me and my family lots of pleasure."

—**Lou**

"I'm a huge fan of your books and have many of them. Keep up the good work! I love your books and eagerly await the newest titles. Long may you publish."

—**Dafna**

"I am a devout fan of your books. The knowledge I gain from reading your books is unbelievable."

—**Steve**

"First let me say that I have been enjoying *Uncle John's Bathroom Reader* since 1994 when I received my first *Bathroom Reader* as a gift. I since purchased the previous annual editions and every one since then. I have also bought several of the specialty editions. I got my grandchildren interested with the children's editions. They are now in college. I am sending them my collection a few books at a time each Christmas."

—**Danny**

"We love the books and extend our thanks to you for all your hard work!"

—**Susi**

Articles in this edition have been included from the following books:

CONTENTS

Because the BRI understands your reading needs, we've
divided the contents by length as well as subject.

Short—a quick read
Medium—2 to 3 pages, but still brief

MUSIC

Short

Medium

INTERNATIONAL AFFAIRS

Short

Medium

CREATURE FEATURES

Short

Medium

FOOD & DRINK

Short

INTRODUCTION

First, a brief history of the Bathroom Readers' Institute: In 1987 a small gaggle of pop-culture aficionados led by Uncle John decided to make a book just for the bathroom. We compiled strange news stories, interesting facts, trivia, history, science, and whatever else we could find to create the very first *Uncle John's Bathroom Reader*. Since then, we've released 30 annual volumes as well as dozens of special editions—books about pets, states, sports, quotes, science, movies, kids' books, and much more. All in all, it adds up to nearly 30,000 pages of bathroom reading. (Really? Wow.)

So why *this* book? Most of our *Bathroom Readers* include short, medium, and long articles—and a few extra-long ones for those leg-numbing bathroom experiences. But over the years, a lot of our readers have asked us to put together an edition with all of the best short stuff. We went back to the archives on this version, and scoured our entire library to find our all-time favorite 1- and 2-page articles (along with a few absorbing 3-pagers). Inside these pages, you'll find the original "greatest hits" and soon-to-be-favorites as well.

Open up *Best of Briefs* to any page, and you're sure to find something you didn't know: an interesting origin, a wise quotation, an obscure bit of history, or something totally random, such as strategies for winning popular board games, the correct use of "compliment" versus "complement," Irish toasts and curses (our favorite: "Your nose should grow so much hair it strains your soup!"), a recipe for Fritos Chili Pie, the winning word from the Scripps National Spelling Bee in 1969, and…well, you get the idea.

So turn the page and treat yourself to a few seconds (or hours) of entertainment. Happy reading and, as always…

Go with the Flow!

—**Uncle John and the BRI staff**

BEHOLD THE SLOTH

Their name is synonymous with laziness, but these small, cat-size animals of South and Central America's rain forests are really just misunderstood.

• Sloths look like rodents, but they're not—they're mammals in the order *Pilosa*, which is Latin for "hairy."

• Sloths spend only about four hours each day awake, and that's spent hanging upside down from tree limbs by their long, pointed claws. They can sleep, breed, fight predators, and even die hanging upside down.

• Sloths move very little because their typical diet of leaves and twigs provides so little energy or nutrition. It also gives them a very slow metabolism. (They poop only once a week, at most.)

• All that roughage is digested by a four-chambered stomach that can take a month to fully digest a meal.

• Only about 25 percent of a sloth's body weight is muscle (most mammals have about 50 percent), and they are unable to shiver in the cold.

• Their body temperature is the lowest and most variable among mammals, ranging from 74° to 92°F.

• The rate at which a sloth climbs a tree: six to eight feet… per minute.

• The sloths' closest relative is the anteater. Another relative: the extinct ground sloth, which fossils indicate were as large as elephants. They were hunted to extinction by primitive humans at the end of the last ice age, about 11,000 years ago.

• The sloth's lack of movement makes its fur habitable to insects, such as moths and beetles, that would fly away from more active animals. Sloth fur is also known to host incredibly slow-growing creatures…such as algae.

• The sloth lives a solitary life… until it's time to breed. In the dead of night, a female sloth will emit a bloodcurdling scream to alert the male sloths.

• Sloths are the only mammals with parted fur. It splits from the belly to the back, which allows rainwater to run off a sloth while it hangs upside down during a rainstorm—a common occurrence.

An average covered wagon train crossed the prairie at 1-2 miles per hour.

(BAD) DREAM HOUSES

Everyone thinks their own horror stories about buying a new home are the worst, but they're not—these are. Note: Some names have been changed to protect the gullible.

Dream House: In 1998 John and Mary Jones found theirs in South Carolina.

From Bad... They didn't get a home inspection before closing. Result: Right after they moved in, problems started. The kitchen sink backed up, the washing machine overflowed, and when the plumber came to fix the leaks, the bathroom floor caved in.

...To Nightmare! Then the air conditioner stopped working. The repairman figured the system was missing a filter, so he went into the attic to explore. But instead of a filter, he found bats—thousands of them. Even worse, over the years hundreds of gallons of bat guano had soaked into the insulation and wood of the structure, rendering the home a health hazard and completely uninhabitable. (Mary Jones developed a rare disease due to exposure from bat guano.)

Dream House: Bill Barnes of southern Maryland was trying to sell his house. Ari Ozman, who claimed to be a traveling salesman who was moving his family into the area, didn't want to buy—he wanted to rent. The market was a little slow, so when Ozman offered six months' rent in advance, Barnes jumped at it.

From Bad... Ozman wasn't a traveling salesman—he was a scam artist. He put an ad in the local paper, offering Barnes' house for sale at a bargain price and—no surprise—had more than 100 calls. And when buyers saw the space, they couldn't resist the deal. Ozman's terms: he'd reserve the house—for a $2,000 cash deposit.

...To Nightmare! He repeated the scam 30 times, collected $60,000, and then took off. Barnes was left with nothing except Ozman's security deposit and 30 angry "buyers."

Dream House: Jack Oldman purchased his in Virginia in 2001.

From Bad...A few nights later, Oldman was asleep in bed when a squadron of fighter jets tore across the sky. He practically jumped out of his

---

So where *do* they sleep? Ornithologists say birds do not sleep in their nests.

skin. It turned out that there was a military base nearby and flight training took place 15 nights a month. Still, Oldman decided to tough it out. Until the house started to smell.

...To Nightmare! Oldman couldn't locate the source of the odor, so he called the Department of Environmental Quality, which found the cadaver of a rotting animal in the foundation (the foul smell was filtering in through cracks in the concrete). What else could go wrong? Plenty—the roof structure was caving in; the chimney was disconnected from the house; and the ground under the house was shifting. Oldman's recourse: He had none—the builder had long since filed for bankruptcy and disappeared.

Dream House: Alan and Susan Sykes moved into theirs in West Yorkshire, England, in 2000.

From Bad... One evening a few months after moving in, the couple was watching a TV documentary about Dr. Samson Perera, a dental biologist who murdered his 13-year-old daughter and hid her dismembered body throughout his home and garden. Suddenly they recognized the house on TV: it was *their* house. When they got to the part that said the child's body—which had been cut into more than 100 pieces—was never fully recovered, the Sykeses packed their bags, moved out that same night...and never went back.

...To Nightmare! They sold the house (at a loss) and filed suit against the former owners, James and Alison Taylor-Rose, for withholding the house's history. The judge said that since the Taylor-Roses were unaware of the murder when *they* bought the house in 1998 (they only placed it on the market after a neighbor told them about it), they were not liable, so the Sykeses lost the suit.

Dream House: Cathie Kunkel found hers in Ontario, California.

From Bad... In August 2001, four months after she moved in, Kunkel had a pond dug in her backyard. After removing only a foot of earth, workers discovered something putrid. "We thought it was a dead chicken," said Kunkel. "The smell was horrendous." The contractor filled in the shallow grave, but the odor lingered. Kunkel and her three children had to move out.

...To Nightmare! It wasn't a chicken—it was a dead cow wrapped in plastic. The development was built on 18,000 acres of former dairy land...and they still don't know how many dead cows are buried there.

LOST IN TRANSLATION

Some years ago, a British company called Today Translations commissioned a worldwide poll of 1,000 professional interpreters to find the world's most difficult-to-translate words. Here's their list of the 10 English words that are the hardest to translate into other languages.

ND THE WINNERS ARE:

10. Kitsch. "An item, usually of poor quality, that appeals to common or lowbrow tastes." (Need examples? Stop by Uncle John's house.)

9. Chuffed. A British word. A variation on the adjective *chuff* ("puffed with fat"), it means "proud, satisfied, or pleased."

8. Bumf. More Brit-speak. A shortened version of *bumfodder*, it once meant "toilet paper," but now refers to paperwork in general.

7. Whimsy. "A quaint or fanciful quality."

6. Spam. The luncheon meat, not the junk e-mail.

5. Googly. A term from the sport of cricket that means "an off-breaking ball with an apparent leg-break action on the part of the bowler." To explain the meaning of googly, you first have to explain the game of cricket—that's what makes this word so difficult to translate. "I am from Lithuania," says translator Jurga Zilinskiene. "We simply do not have googlies in Lithuania."

4. Poppycock. "Nonsense; empty writing or talk." From the Dutch word *pappekak*, which translates literally as "soft dung."

3. Serendipity. Finding something valuable, useful, or pleasant that you weren't searching for; a happy accident.

2. Gobbledygook. Wordy, unintelligible nonsense.

...and the most difficult-to-translate word in English is:

1. Plenipotentiary. "A special ambassador or envoy, invested with full powers to negotiate or transact business."

SAY GOODNIGHT, GRACIE

With her husband George Burns, Gracie Allen was a star of vaudeville, radio, movies, and television…and one of the funniest women of the 20th century. Here are some of her one-liners and comedy bits.

George: Gracie, let me ask you something. Did the nurse ever happen to drop you on your head when you were a baby?
Gracie: Oh, no, we couldn't afford a nurse. My mother had to do it.

George: Gracie, what day is it today?
Gracie: Well, I don't know.
George: You can find out if you look at that paper on your desk.
Gracie: Oh, George, that doesn't help. It's yesterday's paper.

"They laughed at Joan of Arc, but she went right ahead and built it."

George: This letter feels kind of heavy, I'd better put another three-cent stamp on it.
Gracie: What for? That'll only make it heavier.

Gracie: The baby my father brought home was a little French baby. So my mother took up French.
George: Why?
Gracie: So she would be able to understand the baby.

Gracie: On my way in here, a man stopped me at the stage door and said, "Hiya, cutie, how about a bite tonight after the show?"
George: And you said…?
Gracie: I said, "I'll be busy after the show but I'm not doing anything now," so I bit him.

Harry Von Zell: Gracie, isn't that boiling water you're putting in the refrigerator?
Gracie: Yes, I'm freezing it.
Harry: You're freezing it?
Gracie: Mmm-hmm, and then whenever I want boiling water, all I have to do is defrost it.

"This recipe is certainly silly. It says to separate two eggs, but it doesn't say how far to separate them."

Gracie: Don't give up, Blanche. Women don't do that. Look at Betsy Ross, Martha Washington—they didn't give up. Look at Nina Jones.
Blanche Morton: Nina Jones?
Gracie: I've never heard of her either, because she gave up.

…is also known by many doctors as "Stroke Alley."

ANATOMY OF A HICCUP

Have the…hic…hiccups? Reading this page won't cure them…hic…but at least…
hic…you'll have a better idea of what you're…hic…dealing with.

W HAT YOU MIGHT NOT KNOW
• A hiccup occurs when a stimulus causes an involuntary
contraction of the diaphragm, the muscle separating the lungs
from the abdomen. The contraction makes the sufferer take a quick
breath, causing the glottis (located in the voice box) to close, which
makes the "hic" sound.

• Technical term for hiccups: a diaphragmatic spasm, or *singultus*.

• Unlike other body reflexes (coughs, sneezes, vomiting), hiccups serve
no useful purpose.

• Most common causes: too much alcohol, spicy food, cold water,
carbonated drinks, indigestion, or asthma. They can also be caused by
liver or kidney problems, abdominal surgery, or a brain tumor.

• The word "hiccup" may come from the French *hocquet*, which was used
to describe the sound of a hiccup. The earliest known version in English
is *hicket*, dating from the 1500s.

• Hiccup lore: In ancient Greece, a bad case of the hiccups meant an
enemy was talking about you. To get rid of them one had to guess the
enemy's name. The Scots thought holding your left thumb (or your chin)
with your right hand while listening to someone singing a hymn would
stop the hiccups.

• Some forms of *encephalitis* (swelling of the brain) can cause hiccuping.
During the encephalitis pandemics of the 1920s, several cities reported
cases of mass hiccuping.

• Fetuses hiccup in the womb.

• Charles Osborne of Anthon, Iowa, holds the title of "World's Longest
Hiccuper." It started in 1922, hiccuping as often as 40 times per minute.
Sometimes he hiccuped so hard his false teeth fell out. In 1990—nearly
70 years later—the hiccups stopped.

• Folk cures: eat peanut butter, eat Wasabi, drink vinegar, eat Lingonberry
jam, drink a glass of water while urinating.

Icing a burn slows the healing process. Running cold water over it works better.

WORLD WAR WEIRD

Here are some interesting, odd—and creepy—World War I and World War II facts that you've probably never heard before.

The German navy ship *Wien* was sunk in 1918, during World War I. The Italian navy ship *Po* was sunk in 1941, during World War II. What's weird about that? It was the same ship. The sunken *Wien* was raised in 1921, repaired, and renamed by the Italians.

• Nearly 80 percent of all boys born in the Soviet Union in 1923 did not survive World War II.

• "Salon Kitty" was a high-end brothel in Berlin, frequented by German government officials and foreign diplomats in the 1930s. In 1940 it was taken over by the Nazis, fitted with secret microphones, and staffed by 20 prostitutes trained to elicit secrets from their clients. "Operation Kitty" spied on tens of thousands of men until the operation ceased in 1943.

• Penicillin, which only entered medical trial stages in the early 1940s, became so precious during World War II that it was regularly extracted from the urine of soldiers who had been treated with it—and reused.

• During World War I, the British executed 306 of their own soldiers for crimes such as desertion and cowardice. These included 25 Canadians, 22 Irishmen, and 5 New Zealanders. The French are believed to have executed more than 600. The Germans: 48. Americans: none.

• American radio stations were prohibited from doing popular "man in the street" interviews during World War II, for fear that an enemy agent might be interviewed and influence public opinion. Stations were also banned from mentioning weather conditions during broadcasts of baseball games, out of concern that enemies might be able to create national weather maps from the information.

• "Canary girls" was a term for women who worked in British artillery factories during World War I. They were so called because prolonged exposure to TNT causes skin to turn orangish-yellow.

The Manhattan cocktail was invented by Winston Churchill's mother.

• During World War II, the Bicycle playing card company worked with American and British intelligence agencies to create "map decks" that were sent to Allied prisoners of war in German prison camps. Unbeknownst to the Germans, the decks contained special cards that, when soaked in water, revealed hidden maps of routes the POWs could use if they managed to escape.

• At 3:10 a.m. on June 7, 1917, British soldiers detonated 19 underground mines containing more than 900,000 pounds of explosives in a 19-second attack on German positions near the town of Messines, Belgium. The explosions were so loud they were heard in London—140 miles away, across the English Channel.

• In 1938 Yang Kyoungjong, an 18-year-old Korean, was drafted into the Japanese army to fight the Soviet Union. In 1939 he was captured by the Soviets, sent to a labor camp and, in 1942, was forced to fight in the Soviet army against the Germans. In 1943 he was captured by the Germans and forced to fight in the German army against the Allies, making him a veteran of three different armies a single war.

• Russia and Japan have still not signed a peace treaty officially ending their participation in World War II.

• Calvin Leon Graham enlisted in the U.S. Navy in 1942. Later that year he was awarded for heroism after being wounded while serving on the USS *South Dakota* in the Battle of Guadalcanal. A few months after that he was thrown in the brig for three months, and in May 1943 he was dishonorably discharged from the navy. Why? Because he lied about his age when he enlisted: he was just 12 years old. (He turned 13 in April 1943.) He was the youngest American to serve during World War II.

• In January 1943, Princess Juliana of the Netherlands—who lived in exile in Ottawa, Ontario, with her two daughters during World War II—gave birth to a third daughter at Ottawa Civic Hospital. At the request of the Dutch government, the Canadian government legally designated the hospital room "Dutch soil" to ensure the princess would be exclusively a Dutch citizen (and not also a Canadian citizen), a requirement for the new princess to remain in the Dutch royal line of succession. In thanks for its wartime kindness, the Dutch government still sends Canada 20,000 tulips every year.

Ants cannot chew their food.

PLEASED TO MEAT YOU

Uncle John once saw a sign on an electrician's truck that said "Let us fix your shorts." He's been collecting wacky business mottos like these ever since.

Concrete company: "We dry harder."

Taxidermist: "We really know our stuff."

Podiatrist: "Time wounds all heels."

Butcher: "Let me meat your needs."

Pastry shop: "Get your buns in here."

Septic services: "We're number 1 in the number 2 business."

Dry cleaner: "Drop your pants here."

Towing company: "We don't want an arm and a leg…just your tows!"

Window cleaner: "Your pane is our pleasure."

Restaurant: "Don't stand there and be hungry, come in and get fed up."

Diaper service: "Let us lighten your load."

Funeral home: "Drive carefully, we'll wait."

Chimney sweep: "We kick ash."

Trash service: "Satisfaction guaranteed or double your trash back."

Garden shop: "Our business is growing."

Auto body shop: "May we have the next dents?"

Muffler shop: "No appointment necessary. We'll hear you coming."

Car wash: "We take a bite out of grime."

Massage studio: "It's great to be kneaded."

Sod installation: "We just keep rolling a lawn."

Auto repair: "We meet by accident."

Bakery: "While you sleep, we loaf."

Plumber: "A good flush beats a full house."

Butcher: "Pleased to meat you."

Vacuum cleaners: "Business sucks."

---

estimated that a common housefly can have as many as half a billion bacteria on its body.

FREE PORK WITH HOUSE

*Have you ever been stuck in the bathroom with nothing
to read? (Our greatest fear.) Try flipping through
the classifieds to look for ones like these.*

FREE

Beautiful 6-month-old kitten, playful, friendly, very affectionate OR... Handsome 32-year-old husband—personable, funny, good job, but hates cats. Says he goes or cat goes. Come see both and decide which you'd like.

Free! 1 can of pork & beans with purchase of 3-Bedroom, 2-bath home

German Shepherd 85 lbs. Neutered. Speaks German.

FOR SALE

1-man, 7-woman hot tub, $850

Amana Washer Owned by clean bachelor who seldom washed.

Cows, Calves never bred... also 1 gay bull for sale.

Tickle Me Elmo, still in box, comes with its own 1988 Mustang, 5l, Auto, Excellent Condition $6800

Georgia Peaches California Grown—89¢ lb.

Fully cooked boneless smoked man—$2.09 lb.

Kellogg's Pot Tarts: $1.99 Box

Exercise equipment: Queen Size Mattress & Box Springs—$175

Used tombstone, perfect for someone named Homer Hendelbergenheinzel. One only.

For Sale: Lee Majors (6 Million Dollar Man)—$50

Turkey for sale: Partially eaten, eight days old, drumsticks still intact. $23 obo

MISCELLANEOUS

Have Viagra. Need woman, any woman between 18 & 80.

Shakespeare's Pizza—Free Chopsticks

Hummels—Largest selection. "If it's in stock, we have it!"

Wanted: Somebody to go back in time with me. This is not a joke. You'll get paid after we get back. Must bring your own weapons. Safety not guaranteed. I have only done this once before.

Hairobért: If we can't make you look good...You ugly!

Tired of cleaning yourself? Let me do it.

It is believed that "canoe" was the first Native American word to be assimilated into Engl

SWAN SONGS

*When someone dies, whether it's sudden or not, the last thing
he or she did often seems poignantly appropriate.
For a musician, that's often a song.*

JOHN COLTRANE
Date of Death: July 17, 1967 (age 40)
Last Song: "A Few of My Favorite Things."

Story: The man considered one of the most influential saxophone
players in jazz history played his last concert on April 23, 1967, at the
Olatunji Center of African Studies in Harlem. That night, Coltrane
and his band performed a version of the Rodgers and Hammerstein
classic "My Favorite Things," which had long been his signature song.
They stretched it out to 34 minutes in a cacophonous, swirling deluge
of sound, described as "frightening" and "Picassoesque" by both those
who loved it and hated it. Coltrane knew at the time that he was
dying of liver cancer; he'd be gone three months later. The performance was released 44 years later, in 2001, on the album called *The
Olatunji Concert.*

OTIS REDDING
Date of Death: December 10, 1967 (age 26)
Last Song: "(Sittin' on the) Dock of the Bay"

Story: In his seven years of recording, Redding had never cracked the
top 20 on the charts before. But when his song "Dock of the Bay" came
out in January 1968, it held the top spot for four weeks. He recorded it on
December 6 and 7, 1967—just a few days before he was killed in a plane
crash.

MICHAEL HUTCHENCE
Date of Death: November 22, 1997 (Age: 37)
Last Song: "Possibilities"

Story: This song was written by the former lead singer of INXS for his
first solo album, simply titled *Michael Hutchence*. He had been working
on the album, while recording and touring with INXS, since 1995. He

---

n poll: The nations whose citizens trust each other the most also consume the most coffee.

recorded "Possibilities" just three days before his death, which some believe was a suicide; others said it was an accident resulting from auto-erotic asphyxiation. *Michael Hutchence* was released in 1999.

BING CROSBY

Date of Death: October 14, 1977 (age 74)

Last Song: "Once in a While"

Story: Crosby ended his final recording session on October 11 at BBC studios in London with the 1937 standard. Three days later, after playing golf with friends in Spain, he uttered a now-famous line as he walked off the course: "That was a great round of golf, fellas." A few seconds later, he died from a massive heart attack. What wasn't widely known until 2001 was that the *very* last song he sang was on that golf course. The summer 2001 issue of *BING* magazine, put out by the still-active "Club Crosby" fan club, carried an interview with Valentin Barrios, who played that round of golf with Crosby that day. "There were some construction workers building a new house just off the ninth hole," Barrios recounted. "The workers recognized Bing and motioned for him to come over to them. Bing was very happy to be recognized and walked over to the men, who asked for a song. The last song Bing Crosby sang, which I remember vividly, was 'Strangers in the Night.'"

GEORGE HARRISON

Date of Death: November 29, 2001 (age 58)

Last Song: "Horse to Water"

Story: Harrison wrote the song with his son Dhani for old friend and pianist Jools Holland (you can hear it on Holland's album *Small World Big Band*). Harrison recorded it in his home on October 1, in the midst of his battle with throat and brain cancer. With his characteristic dark sense of humor, he asked that his songwriting credit be listed as "RIP Limited."

*   *   *

"We want to be the band to dance to when the bomb drops."

—**Simon Le Bon, of Duran Duran**

How'd they get airmail? From 1939–42, there was an underwater post office in the Baha

MYTH AMERICA

A few things you probably didn't know about the founding fathers who wrote the U.S. Constitution.

THE MYTH

The men who attended the Constitutional Convention in 1787 were a sober, well-behaved group. They showed up on time, stuck it out 'til the end, and were all business when it came to the important task at hand.

THE TRUTH

Not quite. According to historical documents found by researchers at the National Constitution Center in 1992:

• Nineteen of the 74 people chosen to attend the convention never even showed up. (At least one of them had a good excuse, though—William Blount of New York refused to make the horseback ride to Philadelphia because of hemorrhoids.)

• Of the 55 who *did* show up, only 39 signed the document. Twelve people left early, and 4 others refused to sign. "A lot of them ran out of money and had to leave because they were doing a lot of price gouging here," observes researcher Terry Brent. Besides, he adds, the hot weather and high humidity must have been murder on the delegates, who wore wool breeches and coats. "They must have felt like dying. Independence Hall must have smelled like a cattle barn."

• And how did the Founding Fathers unwind during this pivotal moment in our nation's history? By getting drunk as skunks. One document that survived is the booze bill for a celebration party thrown two days before the Constitution was signed on September 17, 1787. According to the bill, the 55 people at the party drank 54 bottles of Madeira, 60 bottles of claret, 8 bottles of whiskey, 22 bottles of port, 8 bottles of cider, 12 bottles of beer, and 7 large bowls of alcoholic punch. "These were really huge punch bowls that ducks could swim in," Brent reports. "The partiers were also serenaded by 16 musicians. They had to be royally drunk—they signed the Constitution on the 17th. On the 16th, they were probably lying somewhere in the streets of Philadelphia."

A red blood cell is about 8 microns wide—less than half the width of a human hair.

LADIES, BEHAVE YOURSELVES

Women, you can follow these antique rules of etiquette…or just laugh at them.

"Immoderate laughter is exceedingly unbecoming a lady; she may affect the dimple or the smile, but should carefully avoid any approximation to a horse-laugh."

—*The Perfect Gentleman* (1860)

"Sending out a letter with a crooked, mangled or upside-down stamp is akin to letting your lingerie straps show."

—*Good Housekeeping's Book of Today's Etiquette* (1965)

"Fingernails are another source of feminine excess. The woman who goes about her daily avocations with blood-red finger-nails is merely harking back to the days of savagery, when hands smeared with blood were a sign of successful fighting."

—*Things That Are Not Done* (1937)

"It's a great idea to file your fingernails in the street car, bus, or train. It's certainly making the most of your time. The noise of the filing drowns the unpleasant noise of the wheels. But it is the act of an ill-bred person. Who but an ordinary person would allow her epithelium to fly all over? I think that one might as well scatter ashes after a cremation, around the neighborhood."

—*Manners for Millions* (1932)

"The perfect hostess will see to it that the works of male and female authors be properly separated on her bookshelves. Their proximity, unless they happen to be married, should not be tolerated."

—*Lady Gough's Etiquette* (1863)

"No matter what the fashion may be, the gloves of a well-dressed woman are never so tight that her hands have the appearance of sausages."

—*The New Etiquette* (1940)

"Don't affect a lisp or talk baby talk. Somebody will probably kill you sometime if you do."

—*Compete!* (1935)

If an animal has a tail, it's *caudate*; if it doesn't have a tail, it's *anurous*.

"A lady-punster is a most unpleasing phenomenon, and we would advise no young woman, however skilled she may be, to cultivate this kind of verbal talent."

—*Collier's Cyclopedia of Commercial and Social Information* (1882)

"Girls, never, never turn at a whistle, to see if you are wanted. A whistle is usually to call a dog."

—*Good Manners* (1934)

"A beautiful eyelash is an important adjunct to the eye. The lashes may be lengthened by trimming them occasionally in childhood. Care should be taken that this trimming is done neatly and evenly, and especially that the points of the scissors do not penetrate the eye."

—*Our Deportment* (1881)

"If a man must be forcibly detained to listen to you, you are as rude in thus detaining him, as if you had put a pistol to his head and threatened to blow his brains out if he stirred."

—*The Gentlemen's Book "of Etiquette and Manual of Politeness"* (1860)

"Still less say of anything which you enjoy at table. 'I love melons,' 'I love peaches,' 'I adore grapes'— these are school-girl utterances. We love our friends. Love is an emotion of the heart, but not one of the palate. We like, we appreciate grapes, but we do not love them."

—*The American Code of Manners* (1880)

"Never use your knife to convey your food from your plate to your mouth; besides being decidedly vulgar, you run the imminent danger of enlarging the aperture from ear to ear. A lady of fashion used to say that she never saw a person guilty of this ugly habit without a shudder, as every minute she expected to see the head of the unfortunate severed from the body."

—*Etiquette for the Ladies* (1849)

"Certain daring necklines have a paralyzing effect on the conversation and even on the appetite of the other dinner party guests, who hope to see a little more than is already revealed and would love to change places with the waiter, who has a particularly stimulating view."

—*Accent on Elegance* (1970)

THE CHEW-CHEW MAN

Where did the low-calorie diet come from? It started with a guy known as the "Chew-Chew Man" to critics and the "Great Masticator" to fans.

THE BIRTH OF "FLETCHERISM"

In 1895, 44-year-old Horace Fletcher was turned down for life insurance because he weighed 217 pounds (at 5'6" tall), and he drank excessively. "I was an old man at forty, and on the way to a rapid decline," he recalled years later.

In 1898 Fletcher performed an experiment on himself. He began chewing each bite of food 30 to 70 times—even milk and soup, which he swished in his mouth—and never ate when he was upset or wasn't hungry. After five months of "Fletcherizing" each morsel of food, he lost 60 pounds and regained his health. He also found that he could live happily on 1,600 calories a day, far less than the 3,500 to 4,500 calories recommended at the turn of the century.

THE GREAT MASTICATOR

The experience helped Fletcher find a new calling—pitching his chewing habits to the masses. His slogan: "Nature will castigate those who don't masticate." Fletcher's lecture tours and bestselling books attracted tens of thousands of followers, including John D. Rockefeller and Thomas Edison. Adherents formed "Fletcher clubs," where they met to eat slowly and chant ditties like:

> I choose to chew, Because I wish to do, The sort of thing that
> Nature had in view, Before bad cooks invented sav'ry stew;
> When the only way to eat was to chew! chew! chew!

Fletcher died from bronchitis in 1919 at the age of 69, and his chewing theories soon followed him to the grave. But one thing that did survive him was his low-calorie diet: In 1903, a Yale University professor named Russell Chittenden examined Fletcher, found him to be in excellent health, and decided to try the diet himself. Soon after, his rheumatic knee stopped bothering him and his chronic headaches went away, prompting Chittenden to launch a series of studies into diet and health. These and other pivotal studies led to a ratcheting down of the recommended calorie intake from 3,500 a day to the 2,000 recommended today.

"What if everything is an illusion and nothing exists? In that case...

JUZT NUTZ

Each year, The Onion's A.V. Club receives thousands of records from up-and-coming bands, some with really, really strange names. Here are a few that we can print (but we can't vouch for their music).

- Dear and the Headlights
- The Dead Kenny Gs
- Human Being Lawnmower
- Happy Butterfly Foot
- Orb of Confusion
- Best Fwends
- The Color Fred
- Tigers Can Bite You
- To Live and Shave in L.A.
- Butt Stomach
- Shapes Have Fangs
- Harmonica Lewinsky
- Earth Dies Screaming
- Shoot for the Stars… and Kill Them
- Secret Lives of Freemasons
- Unicorn Dream Attack
- Chevy Metal
- The Pleasures of Merely Circulating
- Garrison Killer
- Penguins with Shotguns
- DD/MM/YYYY
- Mel Gibson & the Pants
- Doofgoblin
- Ringo DeathStarr
- General Patton & His Privates
- Let's French
- The Shark That Ate My Friend
- I Would Set Myself on Fire for You
- Dyslexic Speedreaders
- Clown Vomit
- Les Breastfeeders
- Happy Mothers Day, I Can't Read
- Neil Diamond Phillips
- Broke Up This Year, Alas
- Juzt Nutz
- If Your Hands Were Metal That Would Mean Something
- We All Have Hooks For Hands
- The House That Gloria Vanderbilt

TOM SWIFTIES

This classic style of pun was originally invented in the 1920s. They're atrocious and corny, so of course we had to include them.

"I've had my left and right ventricles removed," Tom said half-heartedly.

"We've taken over the government," Tom cooed.

"Dawn came too soon," Tom mourned.

"My hair's been cut off," Tom said distressfully.

"Company should be here in about an hour," Tom guessed.

"Where did you get this meat?" Tom asked hoarsely.

"You dropped a stitch," Tom needled.

"Blow on the fire so it doesn't go out," Tom bellowed.

"I suppose there's room for one more," Tom admitted.

"That's no purebred," Tom muttered.

"I couldn't believe we lost the election by two votes," Tom recounted.

"I'm losing my hair," Tom bawled.

"Measure twice before you cut," Tom remarked.

"Thanks for shredding the cheese," Tom said gratefully.

"Please put some folds in these trousers," Tom pleaded.

"I've located the dog star," Tom said seriously.

"You look like a goat," Tom kidded.

"I used to own that gold mine," Tom exclaimed.

"Another plate of steamers all around!" Tom clamored.

"I memorized the whole thing," Tom wrote.

"That's the last time I'll pet a lion," Tom said offhandedly.

"No thanks to that Frenchman," said Tom mercilessly.

"You're not a real magician at all," Tom said, disillusioned.

"I've never had a car accident," said Tom recklessly.

"It's made the grass wet," said Tom after due consideration.

A polar bear can smell a seal up to 18 miles away under a sheet of ice.

PREDICTIONS FOR THE YEAR 2000

For a century, people speculated about what life would be like way off in the future—in the year 2000. Now that it's come and gone, we can see just how bizarre some of those predictions were.

THE DREAM HOUSE OF 2000
"[Using] wonderful new materials far stronger than steel, but lighter than aluminum…houses [in the year 2000] will be able to fly…. The time may come when whole communities may migrate south in the winter, or move to new lands whenever they feel the need for a change of scenery."

—Arthur C. Clarke,
Vogue, 1966

"Keeping house will be a breeze by the year 2000. Sonic cleaning devices and air-filtering systems will just about eliminate dusting, scrubbing and vacuuming. There may be vibrating floor grills by doors to clean shoes, and electrostatic filters will be installed in entrances to remove dust from clothes with ultrasonic waves."

—Staff of the *Wall Street Journal*,
"Here Comes Tomorrow!" (1966)

"When [the housewife of 2000] cleans house she simply turns the hose on everything. Why not? Furniture—(upholstery included), rugs, draperies, unscratchable floors—all are made of synthetic fabric or waterproof plastic. After the water has run down a drain in the middle of the floor (later concealed by a rug of synthetic fiber), [she] turns on a blast of hot air and dries everything."

—Waldemarr Kaempfert,
Popular Mechanics, 1950

The first minute of the day officially starts at 12:00 midnight.

COMMUTING

"[In 2000], commuters will go to the city, a hundred miles away, in huge aerial buses that hold 200 passengers. Hundreds of thousands more will make such journeys twice a day in their own helicopters."

—Waldemar Kaempfert,
Popular Mechanics, 1950

"[Commuters will] rent small four-seater capsules such as we find on a ski lift. These capsules will be linked together into little trains that come into the city. As the train goes out towards the perimeter of the city, the capsule will become an individual unit. One can then drive to wherever he may want to go."

—Ulrich Frantzen,
Prophecy for the Year 2000 (1967)

"A Seattle executive might board his reserved-seat air-cushion coach at 8:15 A.M. It would lift off the roadbed, whirl around an 'acceleration loop' and plunge into the main tube running from Seattle to San Diego. Little more than half an hour later, the car would peel off onto the 'deceleration loop' in downtown Los Angeles. By 9 a.m. the executive would be at his desk."

—Mitchell Gordon,
"Here Comes Tomorrow!" (1966)

THE WORLD OF WORK

"By 2000 the machines will be producing so much that everyone in the U.S. will, in effect, be independently wealthy. With government benefits, even nonworking families will have, by one estimate, an annual income of $30,000–$40,000 (in 1966 dollars). How to use leisure meaningfully will be a major problem."

—*Time* magazine,
February 25, 1966

"By the year 2000, people will work no more than four days a week and less than eight hours a day. With legal holidays and long vacations, this could result in an annual working period of 147 days [on] and 218 days off."

—*New York Times*,
October 19, 1967

Most of Bill Gates's 50,000-square-foot home is underground.

ATM VS. ABM

The U.S. and Canada have the English language in common...or do they?

U.S.: Tennis shoes or sneakers
Canada: Runners

U.S.: Parking garage
Canada: Parkade

U.S.: Rubber bands
Canada: Elastics

U.S.: Candy bar
Canada: Chocolate bar

U.S.: "McMansion," slang for huge generic suburban homes
Canada: Monster house

U.S.: Sled
Canada: Toboggan

U.S.: Flip-flops
Canada: Thongs

U.S.: a fifth of alcohol—about 1/5 of a gallon, or 26 ounces
Canada: a "2-6" or "twenty-six-er"—about 26 ounces.

U.S.: Strippers
Canada: Rippers or peelers

U.S.: Elephant ear (the treat made of fried dough sprinkled with sugar and cinnamon)
Canada: Beaver tail

U.S.: Fire station
Canada: Fire hall

U.S.: Dorm (for dormitory)
Canada: Rez (for residence hall)

U.S.: Garbage disposal
Canada: Garburator

U.S.: Faucet
Canada: Tap

U.S.: Dumpster
Canada: BFI bin

U.S.: ATM (automated teller machine)
Canada: ABM (automated bank machine)

U.S.: Hoodie
Canada: Bunny hug

U.S.: Pond
Canada: Slough

U.S.: Whole wheat bread
Canada: Brown bread

U.S.: Throw or hurl
Canada: Huck

U.S.: Colored pencil
Canada: Pencil crayon

U.S.: Restroom
Canada: Washroom
(But it's really a "bathroom.")

To be called a "heavy rainfall," it must be raining at least 1/6 of an inch per hour.

JESUS IN SHINGO

An unusual legend, and a fascinating place to visit.

T**HE ROYAL TOMB**
If you're visiting the tiny village of Shingo in the far north of Honshu island in Japan, you can take a path up into the woods until you come to a dirt burial mound. Rising above it is a large wooden cross. This, says local legend, is the final resting place of Jesus Christ.

The legend claims that Jesus' brother took his place on the cross, allowing Jesus to escape from Israel. He made his way across Siberia, then traveled into what is now Alaska, and finally ended up in Japan. There, the legend continues, he married a Japanese woman named Miyuko, had three daughters, and lived to the ripe old age of 106. Many people in Shingo believe the legend is true—and the "Christ Museum" next to the tomb claims it has the proof.

The story seems to have started somewhere around 1935, when a priest in the area discovered what he claimed were ancient scrolls. The 1,900-year-old documents were Christ's last will and testament, he said, indicating that Shingo is the location of Jesus' grave. According to a local museum, the original scrolls were destroyed in World War II and all that exist now are copies. But other evidence supposedly supports the claim:

• Although the tomb was never opened, rods thrust into the dirt around it confirm it is lined by stones, an honor only bestowed on people of great importance.

• For hundreds of years it has been a local tradition to draw charcoal crosses onto babies' foreheads, a practice found nowhere else in Japan.

• Many ancient kimonos from Shingo have been found decorated with what appears to be a Star of David.

No serious historian believes the legend, but more than 40,000 people make the trip to the "Tomb of Christ" every year, and many visit with the garlic farmer who owns the land on which the tomb sits—a man who is reputed to be a direct descendant of Jesus. He, like a surprising number of other people in the area, has blue eyes.

Who's George Holiday? The man who videotaped the Rodney King beating in 1991

WHAT'S FOR BREAKFAST?

Some culinary origins to start your day off right.

WAFFLES. Introduced to the United States by Thomas Jefferson, who brought the first waffle iron over from France. The name comes from the Dutch *wafel*. Waffles owe much of their early popularity to street vendors, who sold them hot, covered in molasses or maple syrup. It wasn't until the 20th century that the electric waffle iron made them an American staple.

ENGLISH MUFFINS. In 1875, Samuel Bath Thomas moved to America from England, bringing with him his mother's recipe for "tea muffins." He started out baking them in New York in 1880. In 1926, he officially named them Thomas' English Muffins.

FRENCH TOAST. Really does have its origins in France, where it's known as *ameritte* or *pain perdu* ("lost bread"), a term that has persisted in Creole and Cajun cooking. Throughout its history in America, it has been referred to as "Spanish," "German," or "nun's toast." Its first appearance in print as "French toast" was in 1871.

GRAPE JUICE. In 1869, Dr. Thomas Welch, Christian, dentist, and prohibitionist, invented "unfermented wine"—grape juice—so that fellow teetotalers would not be forced into the contradiction (as he saw it) of drinking alcohol in church. Local pastors weren't interested, so he gave up and went back to pulling teeth. His son Charles began selling it as grape juice in 1875.

PANCAKES. When the first European settlers landed in the New World, they brought pancakes with them. They met Native Americans who made their own pancakes, called *nokehic*. Even the ancient Egyptians had pancakes; in fact, there are few cultures that don't have pancakes of one kind or another. The first ready-made pancake mix came in 1889, when two men in St. Joseph, Missouri, introduced "Self-Rising Pancake Flour." They named it "Aunt Jemima" after a song from a minstrel show.

No permit required: Beavers in Connecticut have the legal right to build dams.

UN-BEE-LIEVABLE

The Scripps National Spelling Bee was started in 1925 and has now become so famous that the winner (and the word they won with) can count on making national headlines and network news shows. Have the words gotten tougher over the years? Judge for yourself.

The 1920s

1925: gladiolus
1926: cerise
1927: luxuriance
1928: albumen
1929: asceticism

The 1930s

1930: fracas
1931: foulard
1932: knack
1933: torsion
1934: deteriorating
1935: intelligible
1936: interning
1937: promiscuous
1938: sanitarium
1939: canonical

The 1940s

1940: therapy
1941: initials
1942: sacrilegious
(The bee was suspended during World War II.)
1946: semaphore
1947: chlorophyll

1948: psychiatry
1949: dulcimer

The 1950s

1950: meticulosity
1951: insouciant
1952: vignette
1953: soubrette
1954: transept
1955: crustaceology
1956: condominium
1957: schappe
1958: syllepsis
1959: catamaran

The 1960s

1960: eudaemonic
1961: smaragdine
1962: esquamulose
1963: equipage
1964: sycophant
1965: eczema
1966: ratoon
1967: Chihuahua
1968: abalone
1969: interlocutory

In 1990 Sacramento, CA, officially renamed its manholes…

MANEKI NEKO

*There are countless superstitions involving cats, most of
them focused on the bad luck that they supposedly bring.
In Japan and other Asian countries, however,
the cat is a symbol of good fortune.*

THE BECKONING CAT

If you've ever walked into a Chinese or Japanese business and
noticed a figure of a cat with an upraised paw, you've met
Maneki Neko (pronounced MAH-ne-key NAY-ko). "The Beckoning Cat"
is displayed to invite good fortune, a tradition that began with a
legendary Japanese cat many centuries ago.

According to legend, that cat, called Tama, lived in a poverty-
stricken temple in 17th-century Tokyo. The temple priest often
scolded Tama for contributing nothing to the upkeep of the temple.
Then one day, a powerful feudal lord named Naotaka Ii was caught in
a rainstorm near the temple while returning home from a hunting trip.
As the lord took refuge under a big tree, he noticed Tama with her
paw raised, beckoning to him, inviting him to enter the temple's front
gate. Intrigued, the lord decided to get a closer look at this remarkable
cat. Suddenly, the tree was struck by lightning and fell on the exact
spot where Naotaka had just been standing. Tama had saved his life!
In gratitude, Naotaka made the little temple his family temple and
became its benefactor. Tama and the priest never went hungry again.
After a long life, Tama was buried with great respect at the renamed
Goutokuji temple. Goutokuji still exists, housing dozens of statues of
the Beckoning Cat.

LUCKY CHARMS

Figures of Maneki Neko became popular in Japan under shogun rule in
the 19th century. At that time, most "houses of amusement" (brothels)
and many private homes had a good-luck shelf filled with lucky charms,
many in the shape of male sexual organs. When Japan began to associate
with Western countries in the 1860s, the charms began to be seen as
vulgar. In an effort to modernize Japan and improve its image, Emperor
Meiji outlawed the production, sale, and display of phallic talismans in

1872. People still wanted lucky objects, however, so the less controversial Maneki Neko figures became popular.

Eventually the image of the lucky cat spread to China and then to Southeast Asia. How popular did the Beckoning Cat become? In Thailand, the ancient goddess of prosperity, Nang Kwak, was traditionally shown kneeling with a money bag on her lap. Now she's usually shown making the cat's raised-hand gesture and occasionally sporting a cat's tail.

In Europe and North America, images of Maneki Neko can be found in Asian-owned businesses, such as Chinese restaurants. And back in Japan, a new cat icon adorns clothing, toys, and various objects: Hello Kitty—a literal translation of Maneki Neko, or "Beckoning Cat."

MANEKI NEKO FACTS

• Sometimes Maneki Neko has his left paw up, sometimes the right. The left paw signifies that the business owner is inviting in customers. The right invites in money or good fortune.

• Most Maneki Nekos are calico cats; the male calico is so rare it's considered lucky in Japan. But Maneki Neko may be white, black, red, gold, or pink to ward off illness, bad luck, or evil spirits and bring financial success, good luck, health, and love.

• Maneki Nekos made in Japan show the palm of the paw, imitating the manner in which Japanese people beckon. American Maneki Nekos show the back of the paw, reflecting the way we gesture "come here."

• The higher Maneki Neko holds his paw, the more good fortune is being invited.

*   *   *

"I don't need a reading lamp in my living room. I don't have a toilet in there."

—Norm MacDonald

Instant classic: Robert Louis Stevenson wrote *Dr. Jekyll and Mr. Hyde* in six days.

BRAND NAMES

You already know these names. Here's where they came from.

Q-TIPS. In the early 1920s, the owner of the Gerstenzang Infant Novelty Company noticed that his wife cleaned their daughter's ears by wrapping cotton around a toothpick. Inspired, he built a machine that made "ready-to-use cotton swabs." At first he called the product Baby Gays. In 1926 they became Q-Tips ("Q for Quality") Baby Gays...and finally just Q-Tips.

FORMULA 409. The two scientists who invented the "all-purpose cleaner" in the late 1950s didn't get the formula right until their 409th attempt.

LEE JEANS. At the turn of the 20th century, Henry D. Lee was one of the Midwest's biggest wholesalers of groceries, work clothes, and other items. In 1911, because he wasn't getting shipments of work clothes on time, he decided to build his own factory. In 1924 he started making jeans for cowboys. In 1926 Lee made the first jeans with zippers.

TURTLE WAX. In the early 1940s, Ben Hirsch mixed up a batch of car wax in a bathtub. He called it Plastone Liquid Car Wax and started selling it around the country. Several years later while walking along Turtle Creek in Beloit, Wisconsin, he began thinking about how his product gave cars a hard shell like a turtle's. "Plastone" became "Turtle Wax."

CONVERSE ALL-STARS. Named for Marquis M. Converse, who founded the Converse Rubber Company in 1908. He introduced the canvas-topped All-Star—one of the world's first basketball shoes—in 1917.

SARAN WRAP. In 1933 Dow researchers discovered a plastic called *monomeric vinylidene chloride*. They called it VC Plastic. In 1940 a salesman suggested they rename it Saran (the name of a tree in India). Dow liked the new name because it had only five letters and had no negative connotations. During World War II, Saran was used in everything from belts to subway seats. After the war, it was marketed as a plastic film called Saran Wrap.

Electric eels must surface to breathe every five minutes or they will drown.

WRINKLES IN TIME

Time travel has fascinated scientists and writers for centuries. While the mainstream scientific community continues to research it, some already claim to have done it. Are they brilliant visionaries, or just lunatics?

TIME TRAVELER: Father Pellegrino Ernetti
BACKGROUND: In 2002 Francois Brune, a French priest, wrote *The Vatican's New Mystery*, a book about how his friend, Ernetti, an Italian priest, invented a machine he called the *chronovisor* in 1952. Housed in a small cabinet (like a TV set) it displayed events from anytime in history on a screen (like a TV set). The user selected where and to what year they wanted to "travel" with a series of dials (like a TV set). Ernetti said it worked by picking up, decoding, and displaying "radiation" left behind by the passage of time. He claims he was helped on the project by Nobel Prize–winning physicist Enrico Fermi and Nazi rocket scientist Wernher Von Braun. Ernetti said he used the chronovisor to visit ancient Rome to view and later produce an English translation of *Thyestes*, a Latin play thought to be lost. He also heard Napoleon give a speech in Italy in 1804 and saw Christ die on the cross. So what happened to the chronovisor? Brune says the Catholic Church forced Ernetti to disassemble the machine because of its potential for espionage.

WHAT HAPPENED: Scientists have never found any evidence that the passage of time leaves a trail of radiation. And the existence of the chronovisor has never been confirmed.

TIME TRAVELER: John Titor
BACKGROUND: In 2000 Titor posted messages on Internet paranormal discussion boards claiming he was a soldier from the year 2036 sent back in time to retrieve a computer to fix software bugs on machines of the future. He made more posts, offered pictures of his time machine and its instructional manual, and gave incredibly detailed accounts of world events between 2000 and 2036. For instance, Titor claimed an escalating global war ends in 2015 when Russia drops nuclear bombs on the United States, China, and Europe, instantly dismantling all govern-

ments and killing three billion people. (Millions more die of mad cow disease.) Survivors group into agricultural communes. Despite the bleak post-apocalyptic landscape, technology is well advanced, with wireless Internet providing all phone service, television, and music. Titor achieved a huge following on paranormal websites and talk radio. Many thought he really could be a bona fide time traveler. But a few months later (in March 2001), Titor announced that he had found the computer he needed and he "returned" to the future. He was never heard from again.

WHAT HAPPENED: "Titor" contradicted himself all over the place, claiming that World War III had destroyed all governments, but also that the U.S. government sent him back in time. Other "predictions" just didn't pan out. He said a second American civil war would take place from 2004 to 2008, and that the 2004 Olympics were the last ones ever held. Also, when asked how his time machine (a modified 1967 Chevrolet, which somehow survived nuclear annihilation) worked, Titor claimed ignorance, calling himself a hired hand, not an engineer. So who was Titor? Some speculate it was a hoax concocted by the late author Michael Crichton.

TIME TRAVELER: Darren Daulton

BACKGROUND: Daulton was an all-star catcher for the Philadelphia Phillies and Florida Marlins during the 1980s and '90s. But he's also an amateur metaphysicist. He claims that a little-known dimension causes all objects on Earth to vibrate slightly, and that only a handful of people, Daulton included, can detect it and use this ability to manipulate objects, the weather...and time. Daulton says that instead of dreaming, he leaves his body every night and travels into the future (but not the past). One event he's witnessed: the end of the world, which he says will occur on December 21, 2012. However, Daulton has also been arrested several times for drunk driving, charges he says he's innocent of. "I've been thrown in jail five or six times," he says. "My wife blames everything on drinking. But I'm not a drunk. Nicole just doesn't understand metaphysics."

WHAT HAPPENED: Daulton was a career .245 hitter. If he could manipulate time and objects, one would think he'd be able to give himself a better batting average.

Tommy Bolt is the only professional golfer to have been fined for passing gas (1959).

UNCLE JOHN'S
PAGE OF LISTS

Random bits from the BRI's bottomless trivia files.

7 People Who Died in the Bathroom
1. Elvis Presley
2. Jim Morrison
3. King George II
4. Whitney Houston
5. Brittany Murphy
6. Judy Garland
7. Orville Redenbacher

6 Things Made with Tallow (Cow Fat)
1. Paint
2. Crayons
3. Candles
4. Soap
5. Shaving cream
6. Lipstick

4 Novels by U.S. Politicians
1. *I, Che Guevara,* by Gary Hart
2. *The Hornet's Nest,* by Jimmy Carter
3. *1945,* by Newt Gingrich
4. *Why Not Me?,* by Al Franken

10 Animals That Kill the Most People Per Year
1. Mosquitoes (500,000+)
2. Snakes (94,000)
3. Scorpions (3,000)
4. Crocodiles (1,000)
5. Elephants (500)
6. Hippopotamuses (300)
7. Lions (250)
8. Cape buffalo (200)
9. Tigers (85)
10. Bees (50–100)

6 Internal Investigations Conducted by the U.S. Defense Department
1. Operation Treasure Trolls
2. Operation Shrinkwrap
3. Operation Hack in the Box
4. Operation Kaboom
5. Project Back Orifice 2000
6. Operation Bad Gas

11 "Lyrically Questionable" Songs Pulled from Clear Channel's Radio Playlist after 9/11
1. "Highway to Hell" (AC/DC)
2. "Lucy in the Sky with Diamonds" (The Beatles)
3. "Hit Me with Your Best Shot" (Pat Benatar)
4. "Smokin'" (Boston)
5. "Walk Like an Egyptian" (The Bangles)
6. "You Dropped a Bomb on Me" (Gap Band)
7. "Burnin' for You" (Blue Öyster Cult)
8. "America" (Neil Diamond)
9. "Sunday Bloody Sunday" (U2)
10. "Fire and Rain" (James Taylor)
11. "What a Wonderful World" (Louis Armstrong)

Huh? Jelly doughnuts have fewer calories and less fat than plain glazed doughnuts.

NASCAR 101

Stock car racing has a rich history...and a complicated set of rules and guidelines. Here's a quick guide for the uninitiated.

How did stock car racing begin? During Prohibition (1920–33), bootleggers in the southern United States relied on fast cars to stay ahead of the law. To maintain a low profile, they souped up their engines and shock absorbers but kept the *stock*, or factory-made, bodies. After a night on the run, the bootleggers would sometimes meet to boast about their cars and race them against each other on oval dirt tracks. This soon became a Sunday tradition, complete with picnic baskets.

How did NASCAR begin? In 1938 Bill France Sr., a mechanic and amateur race-car driver, began running operations at a track in Daytona Beach, Florida, near a stretch of beach where several early land-speed records had been set. The young sport of racing was in trouble, though: Shady promoters often wouldn't pay the drivers, and the lack of consistent car guidelines led to frequent disagreements. France worked to legitimize the sport. After a series of meetings that culminated in Daytona Beach on February 21, 1948, he convinced the drivers and promoters to form a single entity—the National Association for Stock Car Auto Racing. France ran NASCAR until 1972, when his son, Bill France Jr., took over. The younger France ran the organization until 2000.

What's the difference between stock cars and other race cars? Race cars such as Formula One are built specifically for auto racing, while stock cars are made by auto manufacturers for use on regular roads. In NASCAR's early days, the cars were *strictly* stock. But starting in the 1950s, certain modifications were allowed to the engines and chassis to make the cars faster and safer.

How fast do stock cars go? It depends on the track. On *short tracks*, which are less than a mile long, the average speed is about 82 mph. On *intermediate tracks*, between one and two miles long, the fastest speeds top out at about 150 mph. Tracks over two miles in length are called *super-*

Submersible: An iguana can stay under water for up to 28 minutes.

speedways, and there are only two: Talladega, in Alabama, and Daytona, Florida, where the season begins each year. These two tracks boast an average speed of 188 mph. It used to be higher…until a horrific wreck at Talladega in 1987 when Bobby Allison's car nearly flew into the stands. NASCAR now uses *restrictor plates* at these two tracks—a device placed over the intake valve to reduce the car's power.

Why are the cars covered with ads? In 1972, two years after losing the right to advertise tobacco products on television, the R. J. Reynolds Company tried a new marketing tactic by sponsoring the first Winston Cup series (now called the Sprint Cup). In the mid-'70s, partial races were telecast on ABC's *Wide World of Sports*, giving NASCAR a wider audience. But it its biggest boost came with the 1979 Daytona 500, the first NASCAR race broadcast live on national television. On a day when the northeastern U.S. was paralyzed by a snowstorm, millions of TV viewers watched the race—which ended in a dramatic wreck on the final lap, followed by a fistfight between Cale Yarborough and Donnie Allison. After that, more companies jumped on the sponsorship bandwagon, creating a marriage of convenience: Stock cars make perfect blank slates for ads, and stock car racing is so expensive that teams can't do it week after week without the millions they receive from sponsors.

How does the point system work? In each race, a driver receives points for every lap in which he or she leads (there have been 17 female NASCAR drivers). The winner of the race gets an additional 185 points, second place gets 170, third 165, and so on. Because this system rewards consistency over winning, fans complained that the racing was getting too conservative. After Matt Kenseth won the 2003 NASCAR Championship with only one victory (but 25 top-10 finishes), NASCAR implemented a playoff system. Now after the first 26 races are completed, the top 12 drivers' point totals are reset to 5,000, plus an additional 10 points for each race they've won. This means that for the final 10 races, now called "The Chase for the NASCAR Sprint Cup," the top 12 are far ahead of the pack and battle each other for the championship. Adding to the drama: *All* of the drivers still participate in the final 10 races, so drivers farther down in the rankings can often act as "spoilers."

NOT EXACTLY PRINCE CHARMING

Ever heard of Prince Philip? He's the Duke of Edinburgh and husband of Queen Elizabeth II of England. About the only time he makes headlines is when he, as one newspaper puts it, "uses his royal status to insult and belittle people." His public gaffes are so frequent that they've earned him the title "The Duke of Hazard."

To a driving instructor in Scotland: "How do you keep the natives off the booze long enough to get them through the test?"

To a Nigerian diplomat in traditional Nigerian garb: "You look as if you're ready for bed."

On seeing a fuse box filled with wires, during a visit to an electronics company: "This looks like it was put in by an Indian."

To a chubby 13-year-old boy at a space exploration exhibit, pointing to a space capsule: "You'll have to lose weight if you want to go in that."

To a smoke-detector activist who lost two of her children in a house fire: "My smoke alarm is a damn nuisance. Every time I run my bath, the steam sets it off and I've got firefighters at my door."

To members of the British Deaf Association, while pointing to a loudspeaker playing Caribbean music: "No wonder you are deaf."

To a tourist, during a state visit to Hungary: "You can't have been here long, you've no potbelly."

Speaking to British students studying in China: "If you stay here much longer, you'll all be slitty-eyed."

On the "key problem" facing Brazil: "Brazilians live there."

On his daughter Princess Anne: "If it doesn't fart or eat hay, she isn't interested."

Remark to the Queen on seeing a picture once owned by King Charles I of England in the Louvre in Paris: "Shall we take it back?"

YOU'RE MY INSPIRATION

*It's always interesting to find out where the architects of
pop culture get their ideas. These may surprise you.*

CHARLIE AND THE CHOCOLATE FACTORY. In the 1920s,
England's two biggest chocolate makers, Cadbury and Rowntree,
tried to steal trade secrets by sending spies into each others'
factories, posed as employees. Result: Both companies became highly
protective of their chocolate-making process. When Roald Dahl was 13, he
worked as a taste-tester at Cadbury. The secretive policies and the giant,
elaborate machines later inspired him to create chocolatier Willy Wonka.

MARLBORO MAN. Using a cowboy to pitch the cigarette brand was
inspired when ad execs saw a 1949 *Life* magazine photo—a close-up of a
weather-worn Texas rancher named Clarence Hailey Long, who wore a
cowboy hat and had a cigarette in his mouth.

NAPOLEON DYNAMITE. Elvis Costello used it as a pseudonym on
his 1986 album *Blood and Chocolate*. Scriptwriter Jared Hess met a street
person who said his name was Napoleon Dynamite. Coon liked the name
and, unaware of the Costello connection, used it for the lead character in
his movie.

THE ODD COUPLE. In 1962 TV writer Danny Simon got divorced
and moved in with another divorced man. Simon was a neat freak, while
his friend was a slob. Simon's brother, playwright Neil Simon, turned the
situation into *The Odd Couple*. (Neil says Danny inspired at least nine
other characters in his plays.)

CHARLIE THE TUNA. The Leo Burnett Agency created Charlie for
StarKist Tuna in 1961. Ad writer Tom Rogers based him on a beatnik
friend of his (that's why he wears a beret) who wanted to be respected for
his "good taste."

"I DON'T GET NO RESPECT." After seeing *The Godfather* in 1972,
comedian Rodney Dangerfield noticed that all the characters did the bid-
ding of Don Corleone out of respect. Dangerfield just flipped the concept.

CELL PHONE MYTHS

Can you really get colon cancer from butt dialing?
Of course not—that's just a myth…or is it?

Myth: Using cell phones on airplanes isn't allowed because the signal can scramble navigational and communications systems, and could cause the plane to crash.
Truth: The Federal Aviation Administration didn't ban cell phones on airplanes—the Federal Communications Commission did. When you make a cell phone call from the ground, the signal bounces around from available cell tower to available cell tower. If everyone on the same airplane made a phone call at the same time at that same high altitude and speed, the signals would have to bounce too quickly from tower to tower, jamming and clogging cell networks (and making it difficult for service providers to track—and bill for—the calls).

Myth: Cell phones cause cancer.
Truth: Dozens of studies have been done (and continue to be done), and the results remain inconclusive. The largest study, conducted in 2005 by the Institute of Cancer Research, tested 4,000 people and found no link between cancer and regular cell phone use. A 2008 Israeli study concluded that cell phone use caused a 50 percent increased risk of cancer of the salivary glands—located just below the skin where a cell phone touches the face. However, that same year, an Australian study found no link between cell phones and that kind of cancer.

Myth: You have to completely drain a battery before charging it up again, or else the battery will "remember" the point at which it started to charge as its "dead" spot.
Truth: It used to be true, but it's not anymore. In the olden days (the 1980s and 1990s), cell phones were powered primarily with nickel-metal hydride (NiMH) and nickel-cadmium (NiCD) batteries, which had to be completely drained and then completely recharged. If they weren't, the batteries experienced a "memory effect"—the point at which it started to charge up again was its "zero" point. Result: it would lead to poor battery life. Today, cell phones use lithium-ion batteries, which aren't subject to

---

Aw, shoot: It's illegal to use a firearm to open a can of food in Indiana.

the same confusing requirements. You can safely recharge them at any time, regardless of whether they're partially charged.

Myth: Talking on your cell phone while fueling your car at a gas station can cause a fire or explosion.
Truth: Cell phones do give off a very small amount of electricity but not enough to light anything on fire, let alone gasoline. Both the American Petroleum Institute and the Cellular Telecommunications Industry Association have debunked this urban myth, which spread via an e-mail and warning stickers on fuel pumps in the 1990s.

Myth: Cell phones are banned from hospitals' intensive care units because they interfere with lifesaving equipment and electronic monitoring machines.
Truth: It's sort of true. It's been exaggerated…but for a noble reason. Ringing cell phones can be loud; conversations on them may also be loud, disruptive, and emotional, and that can disturb patients and their families. Experts say that only about 5 percent of the devices in use in the ICU would be affected by cell phone signals, but then only at a distance of under 40 inches, and even then, only a little.

*   *   *

NAME CHANGERS

• Sheila Ranea Crabtree hated her first name; she thought it was ugly. She went by her middle name as a teenager, but didn't think that one fit her personality, either. So, with the blessing of her husband and children, the Ohio woman had her name legally changed to Sexy Crabtree.

• A man in New Zealand lost a bet and had to legally change his name. Good news: His new name is one letter shy of the government's 100-letter maximum. Bad news: His name is now Full Metal Havok More Sexy N Intelligent Than Spock And All The Superheroes Combined With Frostnova.

In 2003 New Jersey Devils goaltender Martin Brodeur took…

WRONG WAY CORRIGAN

*While rummaging through our "Dustbin of History" file recently, we
discovered the story of this colorful character. He snookered his way
into the hearts of people on both sides of the Atlantic by heading
in the wrong direction and ending up in the right place.*

T HAT'S MY STORY...

On the foggy morning of July 17, 1938, a 31-year-old pilot named
Douglas Corrigan took off from Brooklyn's Floyd Bennett Field on
a solo, nonstop trip to California. Twenty-eight hours later, he landed in
Ireland...with a lot of explaining to do. He had no passport or papers of
any kind, nor had he received permission from U.S. officials to make the
transatlantic flight.

Safely on the ground, Corrigan offered this explanation to Irish customs: Heavy fog in New York had forced him to navigate using only his
compass. The fog continued all that day and into the night; there was
never good visibility. When the sun rose the next morning—26 hours
into his flight—he was surprised to find himself over an ocean. Taking
a closer look at his compass, Corrigan realized he'd been following the
wrong end of the needle—heading due east instead of west! But by now
he was almost out of fuel; he couldn't turn around. His only hope was
to continue east and hope to reach land before he ran out of gas. Two
hours later he saw fishing boats off a rocky coast and knew he was
safe. From there, he made his way to Baldonnel Airport in Dublin.
His first words upon exiting the plane: "Just got in from New York.
Where am I?"

...AND I'M STICKING TO IT!

He repeated the story to the American ambassador and then to Ireland's
prime minister. By this third telling—to the Irish cabinet—the European
and American press had got wind of the story and ran with it. When he
got to the part about misreading his compass, the cabinet ministers all
laughed and Corrigan knew that things would work out. Ireland gracious-
ly sent him home without penalty.

When he got back to New York, Corrigan was amazed to find out
he'd become a folk hero. In the bleak days of the Great Depression,

---

...the NHL Stanley Cup to a movie theater and ate popcorn out of it.

Corrigan's achievement and amusing explanation lifted people's spirits. Over a million well-wishers turned out for a ticker-tape parade in his honor (more than had turned out to honor Charles Lindbergh after his transatlantic flight). The *New York Post* even ran a backward headline that read "!NAGIRROC YAW GNORW OT LIAH!" ("Hail To Wrong Way Corrigan!").

THE TRUTH

So what really happened? It's no secret that Corrigan's dream was to fly solo across the Atlantic. He got his start in the airplane business in 1927 working for the company that built Lindbergh's *Spirit of St. Louis*. Corrigan helped assemble the wing and install the instrument panel on the famous plane. His greatest honor was meeting Lindbergh. ("Even more than if I had met Abraham Lincoln himself!") After Lindbergh made the first solo transatlantic flight in 1927, Corrigan vowed to follow in his footsteps.

He spent the early 1930s barnstorming the country, landing near small towns and charging for airplane rides to pay for gas. In 1933 he bought a secondhand Curtiss Robin J-6 monoplane for $310, which he named *Sunshine*, and began overhauling it for a trip across the ocean. In 1936 and again in 1937, Federal Aviation officials denied Corrigan's requests to attempt the Atlantic flight.

So it's unlikely that when Corrigan took off from New York in 1938, he didn't know where he was going. Not only was he an accomplished pilot and navigator who had a history of flying without the proper paperwork, but he'd been working 10 straight years toward his dream of flying nonstop to Europe. Wrong Way Corrigan knew one end of a compass from the other.

COME ON, JUST ADMIT IT

For the rest of his life (he died in 1995), people tried to get Corrigan to come clean—but he never did, not even in his autobiography. In 1988 Corrigan took *Sunshine* on a national tour to celebrate the 50th anniversary of his famous flight. He was continually asked the same question: "Were you *really* trying to fly to California?" "Sure," he answered. "Well, at least I've told that story so many times that now I believe it myself."

GOLDEN-AGE
RADIO TREASURES

*Uncle John loves old-time radio shows.
Here are some of his favorites.*

D RAGNET (NBC, 1949–57)
If you like to watch *CSI* or any other police "procedural" show,
you have Jack Webb—*Dragnet*'s Sergeant Joe Friday—to thank
for it. Webb came up with the idea for *Dragnet* after playing a forensic
scientist in the 1948 movie *He Walked by Night*. Other cops-and-robbers
radio shows were mostly flights of fancy, but Webb, the creator and
producer of the show as well as its star, was a stickler for authenticity. He
rode along with police officers on patrol and sat in on classes at the police
academy, soaking up details that he put to good use in his show. Even the
ring of the telephones and the number of footsteps between offices were
exactly as they were at LAPD headquarters.

Things to Listen For: Controversial subject matter. *Dragnet* was the first
police show to tackle taboo topics, such as sex crimes, drug abuse, and
the deaths of children. The grim storyline of the 1949 Christmas episode:
An eight-year-old boy is shot and killed by the .22 rifle his friend got for
Christmas. Gritty realism and attention to detail helped make *Dragnet*
one of the most popular and long-lasting police dramas on radio. It has
influenced nearly every police show—on radio and TV—since.

Note: Good writing is one of the things that makes *Dragnet* so much fun
to listen to; *bad* writing is what gives another Jack Webb radio detective
show, *Pat Novak for Hire* (ABC, 1946–47), its appeal. The endless stream
of cheesy similes ("When Feldman hit me I went down like the price of
winter wheat," and, "She was kind of pretty, except you could see somebody had used her badly, like a dictionary in a stupid family") pile up like
cars on the freeway at rush hour.

MY FAVORITE HUSBAND (CBS, 1948–51)
If you're a fan of *I Love Lucy*, give *My Favorite Husband* a listen. Lucille
Ball stars as Liz Cooper, the screwy wife of George Cooper, played by
Richard Denning. The show was so successful that CBS decided to move

it to television in 1951. Lucy agreed on one condition: Her real-life husband, Cuban bandleader Desi Arnaz, was to play her husband.

YOURS TRULY, JOHNNY DOLLAR (CBS, 1949–62)

Detective series were commonplace during the golden age of radio. This one set itself apart from the pack by making Johnny Dollar a freelance investigator for insurance companies (instead of a typical gumshoe) and structuring the narration of the story as if Johnny was itemizing his expense account in a letter to his client. Each story began with "Expense account item one," followed by another item or two to get the story rolling. The show ended 30 minutes later with the last item on the account, followed by the signature—"Yours truly, Johnny Dollar." The gimmick worked: the show became one of the longest-running detective shows in radio.

INNER SANCTUM (NBC/ABC/CBS, 1941–52)

Before *Inner Sanctum*, the hosts of horror shows were as deadly serious and spooky as the stories themselves. Then came Raymond Edward Johnson, a.k.a. "Your host, Raymond," who introduced each story with bad jokes and one morbid pun after another. He was the inspiration for all the smart-aleck horror hosts that followed, including *Tales from the Crypt*'s wisecracking Crypt-keeper.

Things to Listen For: The squeaking door that opened and closed each broadcast—probably the most famous sound effect in radio history. The sound was actually created by a squeaky office chair…except for the time that someone fixed the squeak without realizing its importance. That forced the sound man to make the squeak with his voice until the chair returned to "normal." Also, do you like tea with your nightmares? For a time Raymond was paired with Mary Bennett, the singleminded spokeswoman for Lipton Tea, who rarely approved of his jokes and always found a way to insert Lipton Tea and Lipton Soup into their conversations. Listening to how she does it is one of the best parts of the show.

THE LONE RANGER (Mutual, 1933–54)

The Lone Ranger was one of the most popular radio shows of all time. It was targeted at children, but more than half of the listeners were adults. If you listen you'll understand why—crisp storytelling and vivid characters make the show a treat. Earle Graser, who played the Masked Man from 1933 until 1941, delivers a wonderfully over-the-top performance—sometimes he sounds like a crazy man who only *thinks* he's the Lone Ranger.

Things to Listen For: Tragedy struck the show in 1941, when Graser was killed in an automobile accident. For the next five shows, the Lone Ranger spoke only in a whisper until the producers found a replacement—Brace Beemer, the show's longtime announcer, who played the Ranger until the series ended in 1954.

THE GREEN HORNET (Mutual/ABC, 1936–52)

The Lone Ranger was such a huge hit that the show's creators, Fran Striker and George Trendle, decided to create a second show by bringing the formula into the 20th century. Like the Lone Ranger, the Green Hornet wore a mask and had an ethnic sidekick (his valet, Kato, a Filipino of Japanese ancestry). The Lone Ranger had a horse named Silver; the Green Hornet drove a car called the Black Beauty. Trendle and Striker even made the Green Hornet the Lone Ranger's great nephew.

Things to Listen For: The show had several announcers over the years. One of them was Mike Wallace, who later became a correspondent for the CBS-TV show *60 Minutes*. One more thing: In the early episodes, the announcer claims that the Green Hornet goes after crooks "that even the G-men (FBI agents) couldn't reach." In later shows that line was dropped, after J. Edgar Hoover complained that *no* criminals were beyond the Bureau's reach.

CHALLENGE OF THE YUKON (ABC/Mutual, 1938–55)

Why stop at *The Green Hornet?* In 1938 Trendle and Striker reworked the *Lone Ranger* format a third time, this time moving it to the Alaskan Gold Rush of the late 1890s, and combining the hero's sidekick and his animal companion into a single character, that of Yukon King, Sergeant Preston's lead sled dog.

Things to Listen For: Yukon King's astonishing insight into the human condition: He growls and barks at the bad guys before they are revealed to be bad guys, and whimpers in sympathy when murder victims are discovered. "That's right, King, he's dead!"

More than 90% of plane crashes have survivors.

MR. T

If you're a fool, don't read this page, as you will likely end up being pitied.

" 'T' stands for 'tender' for the ladies and the kids. For the bad guys and thugs, 'T' stands for 'tough.' "

"As a kid, I got three meals a day. Oatmeal, miss-a-meal, and no meal."

"It takes a smart guy to play dumb."

"When I was growing up, my family was so poor we couldn't afford to pay attention."

"I was born and raised in the ghetto, but the ghetto was not born and raised in me."

"For five years, Mr. T disappeared. Fools went unpitied!"
            —on his bout with cancer

"When you see me now, I'm nothing but a big overgrown tough mama's boy. And I speak with that glee because the problem with society is we don't have enough mama's boys."

"Calvin Klein and Gloria Vanderbilt don't wear clothes with your name on it, so why should you wear their name?"

"I believe in the Golden Rule. The man with the gold rules."

"Anger: use it, but don't lose it."

"Pity is between sorry and mercy. See, if you pity him, you won't have to beat him up. So that's why you gotta give fools another chance because they don't know any better."
            —on pitying fools

"I thought about my father being called 'boy,' my uncle being called 'boy,' my brother being called 'boy.' What does a black man have to do before he's given respect as a man?' So when I was 18 years old, I said I was old enough to be called a man. I self-ordained myself 'Mr. T' so the first word out of everybody's mouth is 'Mister.' That's a sign of respect that my father didn't get."

FAMOUS FOR 15 MINUTES

Here's proof that Andy Warhol was right when he said that "in the future, everyone will be famous for 15 minutes."

THE STAR: Mark Stutzman, a 34-year-old illustrator living in Mountain Lane Park, Maryland

THE HEADLINE: *Struggling Artist Takes Care of Business*

WHAT HAPPENED: Stutzman was just another artist having trouble making ends meet in 1992 when one of his clients encouraged him to enter a contest to design a stamp commemorating Elvis Presley. He'd never designed a stamp before, but he entered anyway, creating a portrait of the King in his younger days. "It's the first thing I think of when I think of Elvis," he says, "when he was really young and parents didn't want their kids to listen to his music."

Thirty artists submitted designs to the U.S. Postal Service; only Stutzman's (a young Elvis) and another artist's (an old, fat Elvis) were chosen as finalists. The American public would choose between the two designs by voting at their post office or mailing in a special ballot.

What happened? Millions of people cast their votes…and Stutzman's stamp won overwhelmingly.

THE AFTERMATH: The U.S. Postal Service ordered 300 million of the stamps and then, when those sold out in barely a month, ordered 200 million more, making it the most popular commemorative stamp in U.S. history. Estimated profits: $20 million. How much of that went to Stutzman? Zero—he got the standard design fee of $3,000…nothing more.

THE STAR: James Carter, 76, an ex-convict and retired shipping clerk from Mississippi

THE HEADLINE: *Ex-Con Makes It Big with a Song He Can't Remember, in a Movie He's Never Seen*

WHAT HAPPENED: In September 1959, Carter was chopping wood with a Mississippi prison road gang. He frequently led the men in singing while they worked, and one afternoon he happened to be recorded while singing a song called "Po' Lazarus." Carter served out his sentence and became a shipping clerk when he got out of prison. By 2002 he was retired.

What happened to that recording of "Po' Lazarus" is another story: It was preserved in a music archive, and in 2000 it ended up in the soundtrack of the film *O Brother, Where Art Thou.* The soundtrack was an even bigger hit than the movie: It went on to sell more than seven million copies, generating thousands of dollars in royalties for Carter... if anyone could find him, that is: After more than 40 years, nobody knew whether he was even still alive.

It took the record's producer about a year to track Carter down in Chicago. One day two people showed up at his doorstep, told him about the movie (he'd never seen it) and the soundtrack (he'd never heard it), and handed him a check for $20,000, the first of what would likely be hundreds of thousands of dollars in royalties.

THE AFTERMATH: About a week later, Carter flew to the Grammy Awards in Los Angeles, where he saw the album win five Grammies, including Album of the Year. For all that, Carter has trouble remembering the lyrics to the song that made him an instant celebrity. "I sang that song a long time back," he says.

THE STAR: Patrick Singleton, the only athlete representing Bermuda in the 2002 Winter Olympics in Salt Lake City

THE HEADLINE: *Athlete Comes Up Short(s) in Salt Lake*

WHAT HAPPENED: Did you watch the opening ceremony for the 2002 Winter Olympics? If you did, maybe you saw it: In the sea of athletes who participated in the ceremony, all properly outfitted for the bitter cold, Singleton wore shorts. Bright red shorts. *Bermuda* shorts—the one thing (other than the Bermuda Triangle) that the tiny British colony is known for.

Even before the Olympics were over, Switzerland's Olympic Museum (where the International Olympic Committee is headquartered) contacted Singleton to see if he would be willing to donate his outfit to the museum. "I doubt we will ever see again an athlete walk into the opening ceremony of the Winter Olympics wearing shorts," a museum spokesperson told reporters. "Everyone will remember, because it was so cold!"

The term "filibuster" is from the French word for "pirate."

SMUDGERS & SLEEPERS

A few bits of top-secret spy lingo.

• **Terminated with extreme prejudice:** When a spy agency executes one of its own spies for betraying the agency. (As opposed to just firing—terminating—them.)

• **Fumigating:** Searching a home or office to remove or neutralize any listening devices, or "bugs."

• **The British disease:** A reference to several members of the British upper classes who betrayed their country by becoming spies for the USSR after World War II.

• **Sleeper:** A dormant spy; sometimes an employee of a government agency who won't begin spying until he or she is promoted to a position with access to classified information.

• **Smudger:** A photographer.

• **Case of the measles:** An assassination made to look like a death from accidental or natural causes.

• **Shopworn goods:** Spy information so old or out of date that it's completely useless.

• **Jack in the box:** A fake torso, sometimes inflatable, that's put in a car to fool surveillance teams about how many people are riding in it.

• **Backstopping:** Creating fake background material (employers, phone numbers, etc.) to enhance the credibility of a spy's cover.

• **Spy dust:** Invisible powder the KGB sprinkled on door knobs, inside cars, etc., so that they could track diplomats and suspected spies as they moved around Moscow.

• **Cover:** The fake identity that a spy assumes to blend in with his or her surroundings.

• **Overhead:** Planes or satellites that spy from the sky.

• **Cannon:** Spies are sometimes paid large sums of cash. A cannon is a professional thief hired by an intelligence agency to steal the money back.

• **The Farm:** Camp Peary, the 10,000-acre facility near Williamsburg, Virginia, where CIA agents get their spy training.

A BARREL OF LAUGHS

This letter is a classic piece of American humor. It's been around in various forms for nearly a century, appearing in dozens of books and movies, and even in a Saturday Night Live *sketch in 2004. This version is a memo to an insurance company, but there are many others. The tale has now been passed around so often that it's achieved urban legend status—in other words, some people believe it's true. It's not. In fact, it was written in 1902 by Will Rogers. (Not really; we just thought we'd add to the legend.)*

Dear Sir:
I am writing in response to your request for additional information in Block 3 of the accident report form. I put "poor planning" as the cause of my accident. You asked for a fuller explanation, and I trust the following details will be sufficient.

I was alone on the roof of a new six-story building. When I completed my work, I found that I had some bricks left over which, when weighed later, were found to be slightly more than 500 pounds. Rather than carry the bricks down by hand, I decided to lower them in a barrel by using a pulley that was attached to the side of the building on the sixth floor.

I secured the rope at ground level, climbed to the roof, swung the barrel out, and loaded the bricks into it. Then I climbed back down and untied the rope, holding tightly to ensure a slow descent of the bricks.

You will notice in Block 11 of the accident report form that I weigh 135 pounds. Due to my surprise at being jerked off the ground so suddenly, I lost my presence of mind and forgot to let go of the rope. Needless to say, I proceeded at a rapid rate up the side of the building.

Somewhere in the vicinity of the third floor, I met the barrel, which was now proceeding downward at an equally impressive speed. This explains the fractured skull and the broken collar bone, as listed in section 3 of the accident form.

Slowed down slightly, I continued my rapid ascent, not stopping until the fingers on my right hand were two knuckles deep into the pulley.

Fortunately, by this time I had regained my presence of mind and was able to hold tightly to the rope—in spite of beginning to experience a great deal of pain. At approximately the same time, however, the barrel of bricks hit the ground and the bottom fell out of the barrel. Now devoid of the weight of the bricks, the barrel weighed approximately 50 pounds.

(I refer you again to my weight.)

As you can imagine, I began a rapid descent down the side of the building. Somewhere in the vicinity of the third floor, I met the barrel coming up. This accounts for the two fractured ankles, the broken tooth, and the lacerations of my legs and lower body.

Here my luck began to change slightly. The encounter with the barrel seemed to slow me enough to lessen my injuries when I fell on the pile of bricks; fortunately, only three vertebrae were cracked.

I am sorry to report, however, that as I lay there on the pile of bricks—in pain and unable to move—I again lost my composure and presence of mind and let go of the rope; I could only lay there watching as the empty barrel begin its journey back down towards me. This explains the two broken legs.

I hope this answers your questions.

Sincerely,
Thomas L.

...discovered this by poking them with sticks.)

FLUBBED HEADLINES

*These are 100% honest-to-goodness headlines. Can
you figure out what they were trying to say?*

Factory Orders Dip

SUN OR RAIN EXPECTED TODAY,
DARK TONIGHT

*PSYCHICS PREDICT WORLD
DIDN'T END YESTERDAY*

CAPITAL PUNISHMENT BILL CALLED
"DEATH ORIENTED"

CHICAGO CHECKING ON
ELDERLY IN HEAT

TIPS TO AVOID ALLIGATORS:
DON'T SWIM IN WATERS
INHABITED BY LARGE ALLIGATORS

**Here's How You Can Lick
Doberman's Leg Sores**

*Coroner Reports on Woman's
Death While Riding Horse*

CHEF THROWS HIS HEART INTO
HELPING FEED NEEDY

CINCINNATI DRY CLEANER
SENTENCED IN SUIT

*High-Speed Train Could
Reach Valley in Five Years*

FISH LURK IN STREAMS

***KEY WITNESS TAKES FIFTH
IN LIQUOR PROBE***

*JAPANESE SCIENTISTS GROW
FROG EYES AND EARS*

SUICIDE BOMBER STRIKES AGAIN

DONUT HOLE,
NUDE DANCING ON
COUNCIL TABLE

POLICE NAB STUDENT
WITH PAIR OF PLIERS

**MARIJUANA ISSUE SENT
TO JOINT COMMITTEE**

*Girl Kicked by Horse
Upgraded to Stable*

KILLER SENTENCED TO
DIE FOR SECOND TIME
IN TEN YEARS

*COURT RULES BOXER SHORTS
ARE INDEED UNDERWEAR*

**Nuns Forgive Break-in,
Assault Suspect**

*ELIMINATION OF TREES
COULD SOLVE CITY'S
LEAF-BURNING PROBLEM*

Karmit Tzubera and Dror Orpaz won a kissing contest in 1999. Time: 30 hours, 45 minu

FOOD SUPERSTITIONS

What can you do with food, besides eat it? Use it to drive evil spirits away, of course. People once believed in these bizarre rituals.

"Sprinkle pepper on a chair to ensure that guests do not overstay their welcome."

"If cooking bacon curls up in the pan, a new lover is about to arrive."

"Eating five almonds will cure drunkenness."

"If the bubbles on the surface of a cup of coffee float toward the drinker, prosperous times lie ahead; if they retreat, hard times are promised."

"Cut a slice from the stalk end of a banana while making a wish. If a Y-shaped mark is revealed, the wish will come true."

"Feed red pistachio nuts to a zombie—it will break his trance and allow him to die."

"When a slice of buttered bread falls butter-side-up, it means a visitor is coming."

"Put a red tomato on the window sill—it scares away evil spirits."

"If bread dough cracks during baking, a funeral is imminent."

"It's lucky to see two pies, but unlucky to see only one."

"A wish will come true if you make it while burning onions."

"Feeding ground eggshells to children cures bedwetting."

"Stirring a pot of tea stirs up trouble."

"It's bad luck to let milk boil over."

"Bank up used tea leaves at the back of the fire to ward off poverty."

"If you find a pod with nine peas in it, throw it over your shoulder and make a wish. It will come true."

"Finding a chicken egg with no yolk is unlucky."

"If meat shrinks in the pot, your downfall is assured. If it swells, you'll experience prosperity."

"Beans scattered in the corners of a home will drive out evil spirits."

"It is unlucky to say the word 'salt' at sea."

Nothing new: The first weight loss pill was marketed in 1893.

PLOP, PLOP, QUIZ, QUIZ

How many classic products and brands can you recognize by their slogans?
(Answers on page 194.)

1. "Good to the last drop."

2. "You're in good hands."

3. "It takes a tough man to make a tender chicken."

4. "A little dab'll do ya."

5. "When it absolutely, positively has to be there overnight."

6. "The beer that made Milwaukee famous."

7. "We answer to a higher authority."

8. "Plop, plop, fizz, fizz."

9. "When it rains, it pours!"

10. "Don't leave home without it."

11. "Ask the man who owns one."

12. "I liked it so much I bought the company."

13. "Takes a licking and keeps on ticking."

14. "Reach out and touch someone."

A. American Express

B. Perdue chickens

C. Packard

D. Morton's salt

E. Maxwell House coffee

F. Federal Express

G. Brylcreem

H. Timex

I. Schlitz beer

J. Allstate insurance

K. AT&T

L. Alka-Seltzer

M. Remington shavers

N. Hebrew National hot dogs

The light above Big Ben's clock face is only lit when Parliament is in session.

RANDOM ORIGINS

*Once again, the BRI asks—and answers—the
question: Where does all this stuff come from?*

WATERBEDS

The waterbed has actually been developed—unsuccessfully—numerous times. The first was more than 3,000 years ago, when Persians filled goat skins with water, sealed them with tar, and left them out in the sun to warm the water. The next time was in 1832, when Scottish doctor Neil Arnott filled a rubber-coated, mattress-sized piece of canvas with water, hoping to prevent bedsores. It wasn't a big seller (even in hospitals), nor was it when English doctor James Paget copied the design in 1873. The main reasons: The beds leaked, and they were cold. But in 1926, scientists at B.F. Goodrich came up with a synthetic material that could make waterbeds both leakproof and warm: vinyl. Sold via mail order, they were, once again, a commercial disappointment. Then in 1968, a San Francisco State University student named Charles Hall was trying to create an ultra-soft piece of furniture. After rejecting a gigantic vinyl bag filled with Jell-O, he tried filling it with water. Hall called his creation the Pleasure Pit and patented it. Waterbeds finally caught on, at least with Bay Area hippies. They became a national fad in the early 1980s.

THE KAZOO

Similar instruments, called *mirlitons*, had been used in Africa for hundreds of years, either to imitate the sounds of animals when hunting or in religious rituals. The sound comes from the user humming (not blowing air) across a membrane, which causes it to vibrate. An African-American named Alabama Vest based the modern kazoo on these instruments. He invented his in Macon, Georgia, in the 1840s. They were mass-produced to Vest's specifications by German clockmaker Thaddeus von Clegg and were first demonstrated at the 1852 Georgia State Fair.

HEIMLICH MANEUVER

Throat surgeon Dr. Henry Heimlich had long noticed the high number of deaths that resulted from simple choking incidents. In the early 1970s, the common method used to relieve choking was a slap on the

om 1889 to 1930, over 3,700 people were lynched in the U.S. About 80% were black.

back. Though it sometimes worked, it often forced food farther into the windpipe, making the choker's situation worse. Heimlich had a theory: a sudden burst of air pressure up through the esophagus would expel an obstruction. He tested it on dogs and found that it worked. Heimlich's "maneuver" forced any food caught in the throat *up*, rather than down, the way a back slap sometimes did. The technique: the person applying the maneuver stands behind the victim with interlocked fingers held below the rib cage and above the navel, and pulls upward. Heimlich published his findings in 1974. Within a week, the Heimlich maneuver was used to save a person from choking. It has saved tens of thousands since.

TARTAR SAUCE

Before there was tartar sauce, there was *steak tartare*, a French dish that consists of chopped and seasoned raw beef topped with onions and capers. Whoever invented it (that person is lost to history) named it after the Tatars, a nomadic Turkic group who lived in Russia in the medieval era and, according to legend, were known for eating raw meat. *Sauce de tartare* was created in France the 18th century to accompany the entree. It consisted of mayonnaise, pickles, capers, onions, and tarragon. The thick, goopy sauce made its way to England in the late 19th century, where *tartare* was anglicized to *tartar* and was served alongside a distinctively English dish: fried fish.

MAD LIBS

In November 1953, TV writer Leonard Stern was stuck trying to describe the appearance of a new character he'd created for *The Honeymooners*. His friend, game-show host Roger Price, was in the next room and Stern called out, "Give me an adjective." But before Stern could finish his sentence—he'd needed a word to describe "nose"—Price responded, "Clumsy." The two found the idea of "a clumsy nose" absurdly funny and spent the rest of the day writing short stories, then removing certain words and replacing them with blank spaces, prompting the reader for a certain part of speech: a noun, adjective, verb, etc. When the stories were read back with all the blanks filled, the results were hilarious. For the next five years, Price and Stern tried, in vain, to get *Mad Libs* published. Finally, in 1958, they printed up 14,000 copies themselves. By then, Stern was writing for *The Steve Allen Show* and convinced his boss to use *Mad Libs* as a comedy bit. All 14,000 copies sold out in a week.

JAWS, JR.

*They're just little fishes, but piranhas can turn you into a
skeleton in a few seconds flat. Nice thought, huh?*

THE NAME. The word "piranha" comes from the Tupi language
of South America and means "toothed fish." In some local dialects
of the Amazon region, the name for common household scissors is
also "piranha."

NOT A SHARK. A piranha only has one row of upper and lower teeth,
not several, as many sharks do. But its teeth are sharper than almost any
shark teeth. When the piranha snaps them together, says one expert, "the
points in the upper row fit into the notches of the lower row, and the
power of the jaw muscles is such that there is scarcely any living
substance save the hardest ironwood that will not be clipped off."
Natives often use the teeth as cutting blades.

FISHING TIP. Piranhas are capable of biting through a fishing net.
If caught on a hook, they usually die from the injury. So a good way to
"bring them in alive" is to throw a chunk of meat in the water. The fish
will bite into it so hard that you can lift bunches of them out of the water
before they let go.

BEHAVIOR. Some things that attract piranhas are blood and splashing.
Experts disagree over whether the fish will attack a calm, uninjured
person, but piranhas are definitely territorial. That's why Amazon fisher-
men know that if they catch a piranha, they'd better try another spot if
they expect to catch anything else.

DEADLY DIET. Surprisingly, only a few species of piranha are
meat-eaters; many eat fruits and other plants that fall into the river. But
those meat-eaters can do exactly what you think they can. In the 19th
century, for example, Teddy Roosevelt wrote about his adventures along
the Amazon. He claimed to have seen piranhas quickly make a skeleton
of a man who had fallen off his horse and into the river.

The Bible was written in three languages: Hebrew, Aramaic, and Koine Greek.

OL' JAY'S BRAINTEASERS

Supersleuth and BRI stalwart Jay Newman has come up with another batch of his simple yet compelling puzzles. (Answers on page 195.)

1. BRIGHT THINKING

Uncle John gave Amy this challenge: "In the hallway there are three light switches," he said. "And in the library there are three lamps. Each switch corresponds to one of the lamps. You may enter the library only once—the lamps must be turned off when you do. At no time until you enter can you open the door to see into the library. Your job is to figure out which switch corresponds to which lamp."

"Easy," said Amy.

How did she do it?

2. MYSTERY JOB

Brian works at a place with thousands of products, some of them very expensive. People take his products without paying for them—as many as they can carry—and then just walk out. All that Brian requests of his customers is that they keep their mouths shut.

Where does Brian work?

3. SIDE TO SIDE

Uncle John stood on one side of a river; his dog, Porter, stood on the opposite side. "Come here, Porter!" said Uncle John. Although there were no boats or bridges, Porter crossed the river without getting wet. How?

4. SPECIAL NUMBER

Math usually stumps Thom, but when Uncle John showed him this number, he knew right away what makes it unique. Do you?

8,549,176,320

5. TIME PIECES

"Everyone knows that the sundial is the timepiece with the fewest moving parts," Jay told Julia. "Do you know what timepiece has the *most* moving parts?" She did. Do you?

6. WORD PLAY

"Weird Nate sent me this list of words," said Uncle John. "He says there's something unusual about them. But what?" Ol' Jay figured it out. Can you?

revive, banana, grammar, voodoo, assess, potato, dresser, uneven

---

Amphibians' eyes come in a variety of shapes, including square or heart-shaped pupils.

FAMILIAR PHRASES

*Here's one of our regular features—the origins
of some common terms and phrases.*

THE BALL'S IN YOUR COURT

Meaning: It's your turn; it's up to you

Origin: "This term comes from tennis, where it signifies that it is the opponent's turn to serve or play the ball. A British equivalent is 'the ball's at your feet,' which comes from football (soccer), and has been in use much longer. How much longer? Lord Auckland used it figuratively in a letter written in about 1800: 'We have the ball at our feet.'" (From *Southpaws & Sunday Punches*, by Christine Ammer)

TO BEAR DOWN

Meaning: To put pressure on someone or something

Origin: "For centuries sailors used the word *bear* in scores of expressions to describe a ship's position in relation to the wind, the land, or another ship. Most are still used by sailors today. *Bear up*, for instance, means to head the ship into the wind. *Bear off* means to head away from the wind, a phrase sailors came to use figuratively whenever they wanted anything thrust away from their person. *Bear down* in the original nautical sense meant to approach from the weather, or windward, side. It later came to mean to approach another ship rapidly, pressuring them to yield." (From *Scuttlebutt*, by Teri Degler)

BY THE SKIN OF ONE'S TEETH

Meaning: By an extremely narrow margin; just barely

Origin: "A literal translation of a biblical phrase from Latin. The biblical source is the passage where Job is complaining about how illness has ravaged his body: 'My bone cleaveth to my skin and to my flesh, and I am escaped with the skin of my teeth.' The point is that Job is so sick that there's nothing left to his body. The passage is rendered differently in other translations; the Douay Bible, for example—an English translation of the Vulgate (St. Jerome's fourth-century translation)—gives: 'My bone hath cleaved to my skin, and nothing but lips are left about my teeth.' The phrase first appeared in English in a mid-16th-century translation of

---

Actor Will Smith can solve a Rubik's Cube in one minute.

the Bible. It did not become common until the 19th century." (From *Jesse's Word of the Day*, by Jesse Sheidlower)

TO EAT ONE OUT OF HOUSE AND HOME

Meaning: To eat large quantities of someone else's food

Origin: "Its first recorded use in English was by William Shakespeare, who used it in his play *Henry IV*, written in 1597–98. In Act II, Hostess Quickly of the Boar's Head Tavern is complaining about Sir John Falstaff, who has been lodging with her, eating huge quantities of food, and avoiding paying his bill: 'He hath eaten me out of house and home, he hath put all my substance into that fat belly of his…' The phrase *out of house and home* was in use as early as the 13th century, and during the 15th century people often said 'he hath eaten me out of house and harbor.' Shakespeare combined the two phrases." (From *Inventing English*, by Dale Corey)

NOT UP TO SNUFF

Meaning: Below standard

Origin: "Englishmen were so fond of finely powdered tobacco, or snuff, that its use was nearly universal throughout the kingdom. Connoisseurs would pride themselves on knowing their snuff. One derided as *not up to snuff* was considered an amateur at judging powdered tobacco. But soon the phrase expanded to any person or product considered to be less than discerning." (From *Everyday Phrases*, by Neil Ewart)

TO PAY THE PIPER

Meaning: To accept the consequences

Origin: "Street dancing was a common form of amusement during medieval times. Strolling musicians, including flute players, would play for a dance wherever they could gather a crowd.

"Frequently a dance was organized on the spur of the moment. Persons who heard the notes of a piper would drop their work and join in the fun. When they tired of the frolic, they would pass the hat for the musician. It became proverbial that a dancer had better have his fun while he could; sooner or later he would have to pay the piper." (From *I've Got Goose Pimples*, by Marvin Vanoni)

First country to issue postage stamps: Great Britain (1840).

FAMOUS TIGHTWADS

For some bizarre reason, really rich people are often the most uptight about spending money. Here are a few examples of people who've gone over the deep end about loose change.

MARGE SCHOTT, former owner of the Cincinnati Reds. Told her staff in 1995 that she couldn't afford Christmas bonuses and gave out candies instead. They turned out to be free samples from a baseball-card company...and they came with coupons inviting consumers to "win a trip to the 1991 Grammys."

CARY GRANT. Nicknamed "El Squeako" by Hollywood friends, he counted the number of firewood logs in his mansion's garage and used a red pen to mark the level of milk in the milk bottles in his refrigerator, both to make sure his servants weren't taking them.

FRANKLIN D. ROOSEVELT. Mooched dollar bills off of his presidential valet to drop in the collection plate at church.

GROUCHO MARX. Wore a beret, which became one of his trademarks, "so he wouldn't have to pay to check his hat."

CORNELIUS VANDERBILT, American financier. When his doctor told him on his deathbed that a glass of champagne a day would moderate his suffering, Vanderbilt —then the wealthiest man in America—replied, "Dammit, I tell you Doc, I can't afford it. Won't sodywater do?"

J. PAUL GETTY, oil baron. Installed a pay phone in his mansion to keep visitors from running up his long-distance bill, and put locks on all the other phones. "When you get some fellow talking for ten or fifteen minutes," the billionaire explained, "well, it all adds up."

LEE IACOCCA, former head of Chrysler Corp. Threw himself lavish holiday parties and charged the gifts to underlings. Popular saying at Chrysler: "If you have lunch with someone who looks like Iacocca and sounds like Iacocca, rest assured—if he offers to pick up the check, it's not Iacocca."

COLD, HARD FACTS

...about the cold, hard continent of Antarctica.

• Antarctica isn't completely covered in ice—98% of the continent is. The ice averages 1.34 miles thick, and is 3 miles at its thickest.

• At 5.5 million square miles, Antarctica is the fifth largest continent (only Europe and Australia are smaller).

• Antarctica is the driest continent. One region has received no precipitation for the last two million years.

• The Bentley Subglacial Trench is 8,383 feet below sea level—the lowest dry location on Earth.

• If Antarctica's ice sheets melted, the world's oceans would rise about 200 feet.

• There are 145 liquid lakes (and counting) beneath the Antarctic ice. One, Lake Vostok, is under 2.5 miles of ice and is about the size of Lake Ontario.

• The lowest temperature ever recorded on Earth was in 1983 at Russia's Vostok Station: −128.6°F.

• Cold, dense air being pulled by gravity down Antarctic mountains create the most extreme *katabatic* (Greek for "go down") winds on the planet. They have been clocked at 200 mph.

• Antarctic ice accounts for 70% of the world's fresh water.

• The largest non-migratory land animal in Antarctica is the *belgica*, a wingless midge (gnat) less than half an inch long. They don't fly (the winds would blow them away); they hop like fleas and live in penguin colonies.

• The Antarctic Treaty, drawn up in 1959, reserves the continent for exploration and scientific research and prohibits its use for military purposes. To date, 47 countries have signed the charter, technically the first arms-reduction treaty of the Cold War.

• Seven countries claim to own parts of the continent: Argentina, Australia, Chile, France, New Zealand, Norway, and the United Kingdom.

THINKING ON-SIDE THE BOX

You probably grew up eating some of these "classic" comfort food dishes, the recipes of which were printed on food packaging or promoted in magazine ads. If you're like us, your feelings range from "Did we really eat like that?" to "I wish I had some right now!"

COCA-COLA JELL-O SALAD
Ingredients:
- One 6-ounce packet of cherry-flavored Jell-O
- 1 cup of boiling water
- 10 fluid ounces of Coca-Cola
- One 14.5- to 16-ounce can of tart pitted cherries in water
- One 8-ounce can of crushed pineapple
- 1 cup chopped raw or toasted pecans

Directions:
Pour the contents of the Jell-O packet into a large ovenproof bowl; add boiling water and stir until the Jell-O crystals are completely dissolved. Stir in the Coca-Cola and refrigerate until the mixture begins to thicken but hasn't set (about 30 minutes). Lightly chop the cherries in a blender or food processor, then add the cherries and their water to the Jell-O mixture, along with the pineapple and pecans. Pour it into a Jell-O mold if you have one, or refrigerate it in the bowl until the Jell-O has completely set. Serve cold with Coca-Cola.

TUNA POTATO CHIP CASSEROLE
Ingredients:
- One 12-ounce package of egg noodles
- 1/4 cup chopped onion
- 2 cups shredded cheddar cheese
- 1 cup frozen green peas

...have all appeared in Japanese commercials for Kirin beer.

- Two 6-ounce cans of tuna, drained
- Two 10.75-ounce cans of condensed cream of mushroom soup
- Half a 4.5-ounce can of sliced mushrooms
- 1 cup crushed potato chips

Directions:
Preheat the oven to 425°F. Cook the egg noodles in lightly salted boiling water until they're al dente—about 8 to 10 minutes. Drain the noodles. In a large bowl, mix the noodles with the onion, 1 cup of the cheese, the frozen peas, tuna, soup, and mushrooms. Pour into a 9 x 13-inch baking dish and top with the remaining 1 cup of cheese and the potato chips. Bake for 15–20 minutes, until the cheese is bubbly.

FRITOS CHILI PIE
Ingredients:
- One large bag Fritos corn chips
- One 15-ounce can of chili with or without beans, heated in a microwave or on the stovetop according to the instructions on the label
- Chopped onions, tomatoes, lettuce, and jalapeño peppers, as desired
- One 8-ounce bag shredded cheese

Directions:
Preheat the oven to 350°F. Pour the corn chips into a baking dish and spread them out evenly. Then pour the heated chili evenly over the chips. Add the onions, tomatoes, lettuce, and jalapeño peppers, then sprinkle the cheese on top. Bake until the cheese begins to melt. Serve immediately.

*   *   *

Man: "Doc, you gotta help me, I think I'm a chicken!"
Doctor: "How long have you felt this way?"
Man: "Ever since I was an egg."

HE SLUD INTO THIRD

Verbal gems actually uttered on the air by sports announcers.

"If only faces could talk."
> —**Pat Summerall,
> NFL announcer**

"Hector Torres, how can you communicate with Enzo Hernandez when he speaks Spanish and you speak Mexican?"
> —**Jerry Coleman,
> San Diego Padres announcer**

"A lot of good ballgames on tomorrow, but we're going to be right here with the Cubs and the Mets."
> —**Thom Brennaman,
> Chicago Cubs announcer**

"Lance Armstrong is about to join a list which includes only himself."
> —**Mark Brown,
> ESPN sports analyst**

"I don't think anywhere is there a symbiotic relationship between caddie and player like there is in golf."
> —**Johnny Miller, golf analyst**

"Referee Richie Powers called the loose bowel foul on Johnson."
> —**Frank Herzog, Washington
> Bullets basketball announcer**

"It's a great advantage to be able to hurdle with both legs."
> —**David Coleman,
> British sports announcer**

"The Minutemen are not tall in terms of height."
> —**Dan Bonner,
> college basketball analyst**

"Jose Canseco leads off the 3rd inning with a grand slam."
> —**John Gordon,
> Minnesota Twins announcer**

"The offensive linemen are the biggest guys on the field, they're bigger than everybody else, and that's what makes them the biggest guys on the field."
> —**John Madden,
> NFL announcer**

"Watch the expression on his mask."
> —**Harry Neale, hockey analyst**

"The game's in the refrigerator, folks. The door's closed, the light's out, the eggs are cooling, the butter's gettin' hard, and the Jell-O's a-jigglin'."
> —**Chick Hearn,
> L.A. Lakers announcer**

WHERE'S YOUR MECCA?

You've probably heard of the pilgrimage to the city of Mecca in Saudi Arabia that is a requirement of the Islamic faith. But have you heard about the Kumbh Mela? *How about the…*

HOLY SITE: Sites around Mecca, Saudi Arabia
THE JOURNEY: The *Hajj* pilgrimage is the duty of all Muslims, if they are physically and financially able to make the journey. It always takes place in the 12th (and holy) month of the Islamic year, *Ramadan*. Some requirements of the Hajj: Pilgrims are not allowed to hunt, wear perfume, have marital relations, or argue; they must walk around the *Ka'aba*—the ancient mosque said to be built by Islam's patriarch, Abraham, and his son Ishmael—seven times. (The *Ka'aba* is the direction that all Muslims face during prayer.) They must also stone the three pillars of *Jamraat*, which represent Satan, symbolizing Abraham's rejection of temptation. More than 2 million people make the Hajj to Mecca every year.

HOLY SITES: Four cities in India
THE JOURNEY: The *Kumbh Mela* is the world's largest religious pilgrimage. It centers around a Hindu myth: Long ago the gods and demons fought a battle over the *Kumbh*, a pitcher containing the nectar of immortality. During the battle, four drops of nectar spilled onto the Earth. Those drops fell in the Indian cities of Allahabad, Nasik, Ujjain, and Haridwar. Every three years a *mela* (fair) is held in one of the cities, rotating so that each is visited every 12 years. *The Guinness Book of World Records* called Allahabad's 1989 gathering "the largest number of human beings to ever assemble with a common purpose in the entire history of mankind." An estimated 25 million people—nearly the population of Canada—attended.

HOLY SITE: Ise Jingu (The Grand Shrine of Ise), Mie, Japan
THE JOURNEY: The Ise Jingu is the Shinto shrine dedicated to Amaterasu Omikami, the Great Sun Goddess and mythological ancestor of the Japanese royal family. In the 600s A.D., Emperor Temmu declared it the most important shrine in Shintoism. At first, only Japanese royalty

In bumblebee hives, the entire colony, except for the queen, dies at the end of each summer.

were allowed in, but it in the 1600s it was opened to the public. Ise Jingu also has the distinction of being one of the oldest—and newest—pilgrimage sites in the world. Every 20 years it undergoes *shikinen sengu*—all the shrine's buildings are destroyed and rebuilt, using the same construction techniques that were used 13 centuries ago. (The next *shikinen sengu* is in 2033.) Today more than 6 million make the trip every year, with more than a million showing up around New Year's Day alone.

HOLY SITE: Chek Chek shrine near Yazd, Iran

THE JOURNEY: Zoroastrianism was founded in the 6th century B.C. and was the official religion of the ancient Persian Empire. Legend says that in 640 A.D. Muslim armies chased the daughter of Persian Emperor Yazdgird III to the mountains near Yazd. There she prayed to the Zoroastrian creator, Ahura Mazda, for her freedom, and the mountain opened up and saved her. A holy spring still runs at the site (Chek Chek means "drip drop"). Every June, thousands of pilgrims make their way up the mountain to a sacred cave, where they pray and drink the water from the spring.

HOLY SITE: Hill Cumorah, near Palmyra, New York

THE JOURNEY: Hill Cumorah is where Joseph Smith had visions in the 1820s, upon which the Mormon faith is based. There, Mormons believe, Smith was visited by the Angel Moroni, who gave him the Book of Mormon—the history of the New World on gold tablets. A huge statue of Moroni stands on the hill, and every July, around 100,000 Mormons come for "The Cumorah Pageant: America's Witness for Christ," during which dramatic reenactments of the Book of Mormon are performed.

HOLY SITE: The Saut d'Eau waterfall near Ville Bonheur, Haiti

THE JOURNEY: Many Haitians follow a combination of Voodooism and Christianity. In 1847, believers say, an image of the Virgin Mary was seen in a tree near the falls. In the Voodoo faith, the Virgin Mary is often associated with Erzuli, the Voodoo goddess of love. Every July, pilgrims journey to Ville Bonheur (the Village of Bliss) and the Saut d'Eau falls. There they stand in the falls and sing, chant, and pray to Mary and/ or Erzuli and other Voodoo spirits. Anywhere from hundreds to tens of thousands of Haitians (depending on political conditions in the country) make the trip each year.

A typical Somali pirate "earns" 17 times as much as an average Somali.

THE FIRST...

A bunch of musical firsts.

...pop album with printed lyrics: The Beatles' *Sgt. Pepper's Lonely Hearts Club Band*, 1967.

...singer to refuse a Grammy: Sinéad O'Connor won Best Alternative Album prize in 1990 for *I Do Not Want What I Haven't Got*. She declined the award to protest the Grammys' "extreme commercialism."

...foreign-language #1 pop song: "Volare," by Italian singer Domenico Modugno. It went to the top of the Billboard charts in 1958.

...double album: Benny Goodman's *Live at Carnegie Hall*, 1938. First rock double album: Bob Dylan's 1966 *Blonde on Blonde*.

...American pop band to tour the Soviet Union: the Nitty Gritty Dirt Band, in 1977.

...musical guest on Saturday Night Live**:** Billy Preston. He beat the debut show's other guest, Janis Ian, by about 20 minutes.

...recorded yelling of "Free Bird!" at a concert: 1976, at the Fox Theater in Atlanta. The show was being taped for Lynyrd Skynyrd's live album, *One More From the Road*.

...music book published in the United States: *Seven Songs for Harpsichord or Forte-Piano*, by Francis Hopkinson, in 1788.

...first African-American recording artists: Pianist Willie "The Lion" Smith of Newark, New Jersey, who played on the 1920 song "Crazy Blues" by Mamie Smith's Jazz Hounds.

...British musician with a #1 single in the United States: It's not the Beatles—it's Mr. Acker Bilk, whose clarinet instrumental "Stranger on the Shore" topped the American charts in 1962.

...band to rock Antarctica: Nunatuk, a band made up of resident British researchers, who performed in Antarctica as part of a series of environmental awareness concerts in 2007.

...album released on CD: ABBA's 1981 album *The Visitors*.

A bolt of lightning is six times hotter than the sun.

PLOP, PLOP, QUIZ, QUIZ TWO

Test your ad slogan IQ, number two! How many classic products and brands can you recognize by their slogans? (Answers on page 194.)

1. "Let your fingers do the walking."

2. "It keeps going, and going, and going."

3. "Come to where the flavor is."

4. "It helps the hurt stop hurting."

5. "It does a body good."

6. "It's what's for dinner."

7. "We love to fly and it shows."

8. "And we thank you for your support."

9. "Rich Corinthian leather."

10. "Celebrate the moments of your life."

11. "Manly, yes, but I like it, too."

12. "Generation Next."

13. "We'll leave the light on for you."

14. "Better living through chemistry."

A. Motel 6

B. Cattlemen's Beef Board

C. DuPont

D. Marlboro cigarettes

E. Pepsi

F. Irish Spring soap

G. Yellow Pages

H. Milk

I. General Foods International Coffees

J. Bactine ointment

K. Energizer batteries

L. Delta Airlines

M. Bartles & Jaymes wine coolers

N. Chrysler Cordoba

THE ♻ SYMBOL

*How cool would it be to have this tidbit on your resume?
"1970: designed a symbol that millions of people
around the world see every day."*

THINKING OUTSIDE THE BOX

The first Earth Day, celebrated by 20 million people in April 1970, not only led to the formation of the Environmental Protection Agency, it also launched an unusual contest. A Chicago-based cardboard-box company called Container Corporation of America (CCA), a pioneer in manufacturing recycled products, was looking for a simple design to print on all of their recycled boxes. Inspired by the success of Earth Day, Bill Lloyd, the graphic designer at CCA, decided to advertise the contest nationally at America's high schools and colleges. "As inheritors of the Earth, they should have their say," he said.

In Lloyd's grand vision, the winning design would be more than a symbol printed on CCA's boxes; it would serve as a symbol to promote the nationwide recycling movement. First prize: a $2,500 scholarship to the winner's choice of colleges. More than 500 entries came in from students all over the nation.

TWISTED

The winner: Gary Anderson, a 23-year-old graduate student at USC. He drew his inspiration from 19th-century mathematician August Ferdinand Möbius, who noted that a strip of paper twisted once and joined at the tips formed a continuous one-sided surface. Commonly referred to as a "Möbius strip," the geometric shape has since shown up in engineering (conveyor belts that last twice as long) and in popular art, such as M. C. Escher's fantasy-based woodcuts "Möbius Strip I" and "Möbius Strip II (Red Ants)."

It was that combination of practicality and art—along with the recycling-friendly notion that everything eventually returns to itself—that put Anderson's design at the top of the contest finalists. "I wanted to suggest both the dynamic—things are changing—and the static equilibrium, a permanent kind of thing," he later recalled. (After the design was chosen as the winner, Bill Lloyd altered it slightly; he

---

darkened the edges and rotated the arrows 60 degrees so the interior of the symbol resembled a pine tree. In Anderson's version, one of the pointy ends faced down.)

CCA attempted to trademark the recycling symbol, but after they allowed other manufacturers to use it for a small fee, the trademark application was held for further review. Rather than press the matter, Lloyd and the CCA decided that a petty legal battle over such a positive message was a bad idea. So they dropped the case and allowed Anderson's creation to fall into the public domain. The three arrows have since come to represent the three components of conservation: Reuse, Reduce, Recycle.

SYMBOLOGY

Although anyone is free to use the recycling symbol as part of an advertising campaign (or as a graphic on a page...like in a *Bathroom Reader*), its use to advertise a commercial product's recycling properties is strictly regulated by the Federal Trade Commission's "Guides for the Use of Environmental Marketing Claims." There are several variations, but here are the symbol's two main classifications:

• **Recycled:** If the arrows are surrounded by a solid black circle, then the product is made from previously recycled material. A percentage displayed in the center of the symbol denotes how much of the product was made from recycled material. (If no percentage is denoted, it is 100% recycled.)

• **Recyclable:** If the arrows are not surrounded by a circle, then the product is recyclable, but only if the "regulations and/or ordinances of your local community provide for its collection."

STILL AT IT

Four decades later, Gary Anderson remains active in the green movement. After earning his Ph.D. in geography and environmental engineering from Johns Hopkins University in 1985, the architect-by-trade has spent the bulk of his career as an urban planner with a focus on controlled growth. When asked how it feels to have created one of the most popular symbols in the world, Anderson tries to downplay his accomplishment, but admits that it's "pretty neat."

GROUNDS FOR DIVORCE

Think you're in a bad relationship? Take a look at these folks.

In Loving, New Mexico, a woman divorced her husband because he made her salute him and address him as "Major" whenever he walked by.

One Tarittville, Connecticut, man filed for divorce after his wife left him a note on the refrigerator. It read, "I won't be home when you return from work. Have gone to the bridge club. There'll be a recipe for your dinner at 7 o'clock on Channel 2."

In Lynch Heights, Delaware, a woman filed for divorce because her husband "regularly put itching powder in her underwear when she wasn't looking."

In Honolulu, Hawaii, a man filed for divorce from his wife, because she "served pea soup for breakfast and dinner…and packed his lunch with pea sandwiches."

In Hazard, Kentucky, a man divorced his wife because she "beat him whenever he removed onions from his hamburger without first asking for permission."

In Frackville, Pennsylvania, a woman filed for divorce because her husband insisted on "shooting tin cans off of her head with a slingshot."

One Winthrop, Maine, man divorced his wife because she "wore earplugs whenever his mother came to visit."

A Smelterville, Idaho, man won divorce from his wife on similar grounds. "His wife dressed up as a ghost and tried to scare his elderly mother out of the house."

In Canon City, Colorado, a woman divorced her husband because he made her "duck under the dashboard whenever they drove past his girlfriend's house."

No escape: In Bennettsville, South Carolina, a deaf man filed for divorce from his wife because "she was always nagging him in sign language."

The Last Straw: In Hardwick, Georgia, a woman divorced her husband because he "stayed home too much and was much too affectionate."

Grate news! In 2008, Italy spent $65 million to bail out the parmesan-cheese industry.

TONGUE TWISTERS

Try to say these three times fast. And pay no attention to the person banging on the bathroom door, wondering what's going on in there.

Who washed Washington's white woolens when Washington's washerwoman went west?

Lesser leather never weathered wetter weather better.

Shave a cedar shingle thin.

Which wristwatches are Swiss wristwatches?

A thin little boy picked six thick thistle sticks.

Flee from fog to fight flu fast!

The bootblack bought the black boot back.

We surely shall see the sun shine soon.

Miss Smith's fish sauce shop seldom sells shellfish.

Which wicked witch wished which wicked wish?

I slit the sheet, the sheet I slit, and on the slitted sheet I sit.

Give Papa a cup of proper coffee in a copper coffee cup.

Imagine an imaginary menagerie manager managing an imaginary menagerie.

The epitome of femininity.

Fred fed Ted bread, and Ted fed Fred bread.

Many an anemone sees an enemy.

Any noise annoys an oyster but a noisy noise annoys an oyster most.

Q & A: ASK THE EXPERTS

Everyone's got a question or two they'd like answered—basic stuff like "Why is the sky blue?" Here are a few of those questions, with answers from some of the world's top trivia experts.

MEN IN TIGHTS

Q: *Why do superheroes wear their underwear on the outside?*
A: "According to Julius Schwartz (famed editor of DC Comics from 1944 to 1986, who edited the most famous of all external-underwear superheroes, Superman), this was modeled after the garb of aerial circus performers and wrestlers of the era. It should be noted that wrestlers, circus performers, and superheroes weren't actually wearing underpants over their leggings, but rather tight underwear-like shorts. As superheroes are generally incredibly athletic and perform amazing acrobatic stunts while crime-fighting, it was natural enough for the earliest superhero artists to adopt this style of dress for their characters." (From *The Wise Book of Whys*)

A LITTLE TO THE LEFT

Q: *Why is the computer cursor slanted and not straight up and down?*
A: "Today, there's no longer a good reason for the mouse cursor to be slanted. But in the infancy of digital displays, angling the cursor solved a real design problem. According to software developer Bart Gijssens, the mouse was first invented back in 1963 by Douglas Engelbart. The cursor was originally an arrow pointing up, but on the low-resolution displays of the day, it was often difficult to make out a tiny vertical line on a screen. So Engelbart decided to tilt the arrow to the left at an angle of about 45 degrees. The angle made the pointer easier to pick out against the pixelated background. Soon, Steve Jobs adopted the left-leaning pointer software from Engelbart, and then Bill Gates snagged it." (Carey Dunne, *FastCoDesign.com*)

SLIPPERY WHEN WET

Q: *How did the Egyptians transport massive stones across the desert?*
A: "The ancient Egyptians transported their rocky cargo across the desert sands, from quarry to monument site, on large sleds with upturned edges. Now, when you try to pull a sled carrying a 2.5-ton load, it tends to dig into the sand ahead of it, building up a berm that must be cleared

---

regularly or become an even bigger obstacle. Wet sand doesn't do this. With just the right amount of dampness, capillary bridges—essentially microdroplets of water that bind grains of sand to one another through capillary action—form across the grains, doubling the material's relative stiffness. This prevents the sand from berming in front of the sled and cuts the force required to drag the sled in half. Artwork in the tomb of Djehutihotep depicts a scene of slaves hauling a colossal statue, and a guy at the front of the sled is shown pouring liquid into the sand."
(Daniel Engber, *Gizmodo.com*)

THE AIR UP THERE

Q: *If heat rises, why is it colder on a mountain peak than in a valley?*
A: "Heat doesn't rise. Low density air rises if surrounded by air of higher density. Air that's heated by contact with the warm ground becomes less dense and therefore rises. As it rises, it mixes with cooler air above and cools to a point where it stops rising. Air at the top of a mountain makes little contact with the ground and is therefore cold. Air in the valley below makes a great deal of contact and is therefore warm." (From *The Last Word*, published by *New Scientist* magazine)

PULP FACT

Q: *What was in the mysterious glowing briefcase in* Pulp Fiction?
A: "After many Answer Man discussions on the briefcase, I received the following from Roger Avary, who co-wrote the film with Quentin Tarantino: 'Originally the briefcase contained diamonds. But that just seemed too boring and predictable. So it was decided that the contents were never to be seen. That way each audience member will fill in the "blank" with their own ultimate contents. All you were supposed to know is that it was "so beautiful." No prop master can come up with something better than each individual's imagination. Then somebody had the bright idea (which I think was a mistake) of putting an orange light bulb in there. Suddenly what could have been anything became anything super-natural. Didn't need to push the effect.'" (From *Questions for the Movie Answer Man*, by Roger Ebert)

According to German folklore, Great Danes were once used to guard against evil spirits.

CRAZY EIGHTS

This page originally explained the meaning of life, but our dog eight it.

THE KIDS ON *EIGHT IS ENOUGH*
Mary
(Lani O'Grady)
Joanie
(Laurie Walters)
Nancy
(Dianne Kay)
Elizabeth
(Connie Needham)
Susan
(Susan Richardson)
David
(Grant Goodeve)
Tommy
(Willie Aames)
Nicholas
(Adam Rich)

DEFUNCT OLYMPIC SPORTS
Tug-of-war, Golf,
Rugby, Croquet, Polo,
Lacrosse, Waterskiing,
Power boating

THE IVY LEAGUE
Harvard, Brown, Yale,
Cornell, Dartmouth,
Princeton, Columbia,
University of
Pennsylvania

U.S. PRESIDENTS FROM VIRGINIA
George Washington
Thomas Jefferson
James Madison
John Tyler
James Monroe
Zachary Taylor
Woodrow Wilson
William H. Harrison

LONGEST RIVERS IN NORTH AMERICA
Missouri
(2,500 miles)
Mississippi
(2,330 miles)
Rio Grande
(1,885 miles)
Colorado
(1,450 miles)
Yukon
(1,265 miles)
Mackenzie
(1,250 miles)
Columbia
(1,152 miles)
Churchill
(1,000 miles)

GR8 MUSICIANS WHO NEVER WON A GRAMMY
The Doors
Diana Ross
Led Zeppelin
Jimi Hendrix
Chuck Berry
Patsy Cline
The Beach Boys
Sam Cooke

MOST POPULAR ICE CREAM FLAVORS
Vanilla
Chocolate
Butter pecan
Strawberry
Neapolitan
Chocolate chip
French vanilla
Cookies and cream

THE PARTS OF SPEECH
Noun, Verb,
Adjective, Adverb,
Pronoun, Preposition,
Conjunction,
Interjection

The USDA once paid $46,000 for a study on how long it took Americans to cook break

VAMPIRES ON BIKINI BEACH

Film historian David Skal writes, "Dracula has been depicted in film more times than almost any fictional being." Here's a look at some of the more unusual vampire movies that have been made.

Dracula Blows His Cool (1982)
"Three voluptuous models and their photographer restore an ancient castle and open a disco in it. The vampire lurking about the castle welcomes the party with his fangs."
(*Video Hound's Golden Movie Retriever 2001*)

Little Red Riding Hood and Tom Thumb vs. the Monsters (1960)
"Little Red Riding Hood and Tom Thumb fight a vampire and a witch in a haunted forest! One of three Hood movies made the same year in Mexico and shipped up here like clockwork in the mid-'60s to warp the minds of little kids whose parents wanted to go Christmas shopping."
(*The Psychotronic Encyclopedia of Film*)

Planet of the Vampires (1965)
"Some astronauts crash land on a strange planet where the undead kill the living, only to discover that the alien-possessed vampiric survivors are preparing to land on another alien world—Earth!"
(*The Essential Monster Movie Guide*)

The Devil Bat (1940)
"Bela Lugosi plays a crazed scientist who trains bats to kill at the scent of a certain perfume." (*Halliwell's Film and Video Guide*)

Haunted Cop Shop (1984)
"When vampires invade a meat-packing plant, the elite Monster Police Squad is brought in to stop them. When the squad botches the job, the Police Commissioner bumps them down to foot patrol until the vampires

attack the county hospital. Impressive special effects."
(*The Illustrated Vampire Movie Guide*)

Samson vs. the Vampire Women (1961)
"Sexy vampire women keep muscular male slaves on slabs in their atmospheric crypt. Santo the silver-masked Mexican wrestling hero (called Samson in the dubbed version) defeats them all."
(*The Psychotronic Encyclopedia of Film*)

Vampires on Bikini Beach (1988)
"Californians save their beach from undesirable vampires." (Is there some other kind?) (*The Illustrated Vampire Movie Guide*)

Billy the Kid vs. Dracula (1965)
"The title says it all. Dracula travels to the Old West, anxious to put the bite on a pretty lady ranch owner. Her fiancé, the legendary Billy the Kid, steps in to save his girl from becoming a vampire herself. A classic."
(*Video Hound's Golden Movie Retriever*)

The Return of the Vampire (1943)
"Bela Lugosi plays Armand Tesla (basically Dracula under another name), who returns to claim a girl after 'marking' her when she was a child. But his assistant, the werewolf-with-a-heart, turns on him and drags him out into the sunlight, where he melts in spectacular fashion."
(*Amazon Reviews*)

Atom Age Vampire (1960)
"Badly dubbed Italian timewaster with cheese-ball special effects and a tired premise. A mad professor restores the face of a scarred accident victim." (*Video Movie Guide*)

Haunted Cop Shop II (1986)
"This improved sequel to the 1984 original features non-stop action. The vampire creature is destroyed by the hero relieving himself into a swimming pool and completing an electrical circuit!"
(*The Illustrated Vampire Movie Guide*)

"DID I SHAVE MY LEGS FOR THIS?"

…and other great—and real—country song titles.

"Mama Get a Hammer (There's a Fly on Papa's Head)"

"Rednecks, White Socks, and Blue Ribbon Beer"

"He Went to Sleep and the Hogs Ate Him"

"Redneck Martians Stole My Baby"

"If Fingerprints Showed Up on Skin, Wonder Whose I'd Find on You"

"It Ain't Love, but It Ain't Bad"

"Flushed from the Bathroom of Your Heart"

"She Feels Like a Brand New Man Tonight"

"She Got the Gold Mine (I Got the Shaft)"

"You're the Reason Our Kids Are Ugly"

"She Dropped Me in Denver (So I Had a Whole Mile to Fall)"

"Thank God and Greyhound She's Gone"

"She Broke My Heart at Walgreens (and I Cried All the Way to Sears)"

"Get Your Tongue Outta My Mouth (Cause I'm Kissing You Goodbye)"

"All My Exes Live in Texas (That's Why I Hang My Hat in Tennessee)"

"I Got in at Two With a Ten and Woke Up at Ten With a Two"

"Touch Me with More Than Your Hands"

"My Wife Left Me for My Girlfriend"

"Get Your Biscuits in the Oven and Your Buns in the Bed"

"Drop-Kick Me, Jesus, Through the Goalposts of Life"

"I'm the Only Hell (My Mama Ever Raised)"

"Too Dumb for New York, Too Ugly for L.A."

"If You See Me Gettin' Smaller, It's 'Cause I'm Leavin' You"

All you can eat: A single Alaskan King Crab can yield over 6 pounds of meat.

LATE BLOOMERS

Sometimes it seems like child prodigies and teenage phenoms are a dime a dozen. But, as these people prove, it's never too late to become a spectacular success.

L**ATE BLOOMER:** Clara Peller

STORY: Peller was a 74-year-old manicurist when a television crew member plucked her out of her salon and asked her to appear as an extra in a commercial—as a manicurist. Eight years later, the commercial's producer remembered Peller when he was casting a series of ads for Wendy's hamburgers. He located her—now 82 and retired from her nail salon—and gave her a role as a grumpy old lady with a catchphrase: "Where's the beef?" Peller's one-line performance was a hit. In the final three years of her life, she worked in commercials and movies, and even made an appearance on *Saturday Night Live*.

LATE BLOOMER: Helen Hooven Santmyer

STORY: Santmyer, born in 1895, always wanted to be a writer. By the age of 33 she'd published two novels, but neither was a commercial success. That wouldn't come for another 55 years when, at the age of 88, she published her landmark novel *…And Ladies of the Club*. The book, which had taken her nearly 10 years to write (and a year and a half to condense down to 1,300 pages), became a runaway success, selling more than a million copies and spending eight months on the *New York Times* bestseller list.

LATE BLOOMER: Jacob Cohen

STORY: At the age of 19, Cohen was determined to become a comedian. But after struggling for nine years, he gave up—he needed a real job to support his family. He worked odd jobs (including selling aluminum siding) until his 40s, when he decided to give show business a second try. Cohen went on to have a very respectable 40-year career in television and films under the name Rodney Dangerfield.

A 1792 law made coin defacement, counterfeiting, and embezzlement...

CHOKE AND CROAK

It figures that an industry as mistrusted as car sales would have its own slanguage. See how many of these expressions you overhear the next time you're in the market for a car.

Monroney: The window sticker on a new car (named for U.S. senator Mike Monroney, who authored the 1958 legislation that requires them)

Third Baseman: Someone who accompanies a potential car buyer because they're unable to negotiate the sale by themselves

Be-back: A potential buyer who leaves the lot without buying anything, but who promises he'll "be back"

Be-back Bus: A mythical vehicle that will someday deliver all the customers who said they'd be back

Whiskers: A car that's been sitting on the lot for a very long time

Hit Everything but the Lottery: A car with lots of dents, dings, and scrapes

Handshaker: A car with a manual transmission (a stick shift)

Bone Thrower: A sunroof

Toad: A worthless trade-in vehicle (it'll be sold for scrap)

Buried: A customer who owes more on his (or her) trade-in vehicle than it's worth

Broom 'em: Getting a non-buying customer off the lot so that he doesn't waste a salesperson's time

Choke and Croak: Disability and life insurance policies that dealerships try to include in a sale

Mooch: A customer who insists on buying the car at the dealer's invoice price.

Mop-and-Glow: Paint sealer (an add-on sold to buyers to increase the dealer's profit)

Unhorse or Dehorse: Hiding a buyer's trade-in vehicle to keep him from leaving

Friday Car: A car with a lot of mechanical problems. (It must have been manufactured on a Friday, when the auto workers were rushing to start the weekend.)

...by U.S. Mint employees punishable by death.

HOW TO WIN AT BOARD GAMES

*Playing board games like Scrabble or Risk against a skilled
player can be aggravating. Here are a few devious tactics
and tips that may help you win (almost) every time.*

MONOPOLY

Tournament players often employ an aggressive strategy at the beginning
of their matches. They purchase every property they land on. Then, after
a little wheeling and dealing with other players to obtain all the properties
of a single color, they start placing houses on their squares. (The cheaper
ones first, because funds are typically low early in the game.) Opinions vary
on which properties are landed on the most often, but many swear it's the
orange ones. Buying as many of those as possible should be considered a
priority, because the more property you own there, the more you get to
collect in rent from the other players. Late in the game, it pays to stay in
jail for as long as possible. That way you can collect rent on your properties
while you remain safely behind bars, away from your opponents' rent-
earning properties.

BATTLESHIP

When setting up your ships at the beginning of the game, it helps to place
smaller vessels alongside or beneath larger ones. You should also put at least
one ship on the edge of your board, since most players tend to aim for the
middle. Another tip: never fire another peg within one space of a miss. This
will help reduce your need to randomly guess where your opponent's ships
are hiding by at least half. There's also the "checkerboard method," which
involves imagining the board with alternating black-and-white squares and
firing only on the black ones. Then, once you score a hit, you should fire
pegs adjacently until you sink your opponent's boat.

THE GAME OF LIFE

At the beginning of the game, you should probably go to college. This will
help you get a better job and earn a higher salary, although doing so might
not help if you don't land on enough "Pay Day" squares later on. Auto and

---

Motto of Springfield, the town in *The Simpsons*: "A noble spirit embiggens the smallest m

home insurance can come in handy, but unless you're really unlucky, you'll be throwing away your hard-earned play money. Instead, invest in stocks. If you land on a "Lucky Day" square, you should always gamble instead of keeping the initial jackpot—the chances of winning are around 5 to 1.

SCRABBLE

You don't need a huge vocabulary to win at Scrabble, but it does help to know a lot of the obscure, two-letter words to use late in the game where there isn't a lot of space available for longer words. First, there's "za." Definition: "pizza." "Qi" is another simple but powerful word. (It means "life force.") And don't be afraid to swap out all your letters if you wind up with a tray full of lousy ones. Yes, you lose a turn, but it will likely aid you in the long run. Another key tactic: play defensively. Don't create words that will allow your opponents to capitalize on the triple-letter or triple-word squares. Oh, and there's one more word you should memorize: "oxyphenbutazone." It's an anti-inflammatory drug, and, theoretically, the highest-scoring word possible in Scrabble. It could earn as many as 1,778 points.

RISK

Since the late 1950s, the "Game of Global Domination" has brought out the power-hungry dictator in millions. If full-scale warfare isn't your forte, follow these tips the next time you play, and end the game quickly. At the game's outset, focus on taking over every territory in Australia and South America—two remote continents that are easy to defend—as quickly as possible. This will earn you some "continent bonuses" that will significantly boost the number of armies at your disposal. Then allow several turns to pass while your opponents attack each other. Once your forces grow big enough, launch your own invasions. It goes without saying that when you attack a territory, do so with as many armies as possible. Why? Because if you win the battle with just a few armies, you probably won't have enough left to protect the territory you invaded. Also, learn a lesson from Napoleon: don't attempt to invade both Europe and Asia at the same time.

*   *   *

"What I learned from losing: winning's better." —**Ted Turner**

You swallow about a liter of mucus every day.

FART FACTS

You won't find trivia like this in any ordinary book.

THE NAME

The word *fart* comes from the Old English term *foertan*, to explode. *Foertan* is also the origin of the word *petard*, an early type of bomb. *Petard*, in turn, is the origin of a more obscure term for fart—*ped*, or *pet*, which was once used by military men. (In Shakespeare's *Henry IV*, there's a character whose name means fart—Peto.)

WHY DO YOU FART?

Flatulence has many causes—for example, swallowing air as you eat and lactose intolerance. (Lactose is a sugar molecule in milk, and many people lack the enzyme needed to digest it.) But the most common cause is food that ferments in the gastrointestinal tract.

• A simple explanation: The fats, proteins, and carbohydrates you eat become a "gastric soup" in your stomach. This soup then passes into the small intestine, where much of it is absorbed through the intestinal walls into the bloodstream to feed the body.

• But the small intestine can't absorb everything, especially complex carbohydrates. Some complex carbohydrates—the ones made up of several sugar molecules (beans, some milk products, fiber) can't be broken down. So they're simply passed along to the colon, where bacteria living in your intestine feed off the fermenting brew. If that sounds gross, try this: The bacteria then excrete gases into your colon. Farting is how your colon rids itself of the pressure the gas creates.

FRUIT OF THE VINE

So why not just quit eating complex carbohydrates?

• First, complex carbohydrates—which include fruit, vegetables, and whole grains—are crucial for a healthy diet. "Put it this way," explains Jeff Rank, an associate professor of gastroenterology at the University of Minnesota. "Cabbage and beans are bad for gas, but they are good for you."

A *klaxon* is an electric horn. The name comes from a German word meaning "shriek."

• Second, they're not the culprits when it comes to the least desirable aspect of farting: smell.

• Farts are about 99% odorless gases—hydrogen, nitrogen, carbon dioxide, oxygen, and methane (it's the methane that makes farts flammable). So why the odor? Blame it on those millions of bacteria living in your colon. Their waste gases usually contain sulfur molecules—which smell like rotten eggs. This is the remaining 1% that clears rooms in a hurry.

AM I NORMAL?

• Johnson & Johnson, which produces drugs for gas and indigestion, once conducted a survey and found that almost one-third of Americans believe they have a flatulence problem.

• However, according to Terry Bolin and Rosemary Stanton, authors of *Wind Breaks: Coming to Terms with Flatulence*, doctors say most flatulence is healthy. What's unhealthy is worrying about it so much.

NOTABLE FARTERS

• Le Petomane, a 19th-century music hall performer, had the singular ability to control his farts. He could play tunes, as well as imitate animal and machinery sounds rectally. Le Petomane's popularity briefly rivaled that of Sarah Bernhardt.

• A computer factory in England, built on the site of a 19th-century chapel, is reportedly inhabited by a farting ghost. Workers think it might be the embarrassed spirit of a girl who farted while singing in church. "On several occasions," said an employee, "there has been a faint girlish voice singing faint hymns, followed by a loud raspberry sound and then a deathly hush."

• Josef Stalin was afraid of farting in public. He kept glasses and a water pitcher on his desk so that if he felt a wind coming on, he could mask the sound by clinking the glasses while pouring water.

• Martin Luther believed, "On the basis of personal experience, farts could scare off Satan himself."

*   *   *

"Why doesn't Tarzan have a beard?" —**George Carlin**

YAH-HAH, EVIL SPIDER WOMAN!

Until recently, law required all movies made in Hong Kong to have English subtitles. But producers spent as little on translations as possible…and it shows. These gems are actual subtitles from action movies.

"Take my advice, or I'll spank you without pants."

"Fatty, you with your thick face have hurt my instep."

"You always use violence. I should've ordered glutinous rice chicken."

"Who gave you the nerve to get killed here?"

"This will be of fine service for you, you bag of the scum. I am sure you will not mind that I remove your toenails and leave them out on the dessert floor for ants to eat."

"A normal person wouldn't steal pituitaries."

"That may disarray my intestines."

"The bullets inside are very hot. Why do I feel so cold?"

"Beware! Your bones are going to be disconnected."

"I am darn unsatisfied to be killed in this way."

"If you don't eat people, they'll eat you."

"She's terrific. I can't stand her."

"Darn, I'll burn you into a BBQ chicken."

"I'll cut your fats out, don't you believe it?"

"Sex fiend, you'll never get reincarnated!"

"How can I make love without TV?"

"I got knife scars more than the number of your leg's hair!"

"Yah-hah, evil spider woman! I have captured you by the short rabbits and can now deliver you violently to your doctor for a thorough extermination."

"What is a soul? It's just a toilet paper."

House dust can vary in composition from room to room.

FILTHY WATER PEOPLE

*Did you ever get a lousy nickname that stuck? You're
in good company. Many Native American tribes are
known today by unflattering names given to them
by their neighbors. Here are a few examples.*

CHEYENNE

Meaning: Red-Talkers

Origin: This Great Plains tribe called themselves the
Tsitsistas, which means the "Beautiful People." The neighboring Dakota
people may have agreed, but they couldn't understand what the Tsitsistas
were saying, because they spoke a different language. They called the Tsitsistas the "Red-Talkers," meaning "those who speak unintelligibly," or, in
Dakota, the *Cheyenne*.

APACHE

Meaning: Enemy

Origin: Like many Native American tribes, this one, famous for legendary
chief Geronimo, called themselves "the People"—*Dine* (di-nay) in their
native language. But the neighboring tribe—victim of many of their war
parties—the Zuni, called them "the enemy," or *apachu*. Over time, that
evolved into their permanent name, the *Apache*.

ARAPAHO

Meaning: Tattooed People

Origin: These Plains Indians called themselves the *Inuna-ina*, which
translates to "the People." Their neighbors, the Crow, identified them by
their distinctive body markings and called them "Tattooed People," or, in
their language, *Arapahos*.

HURON

Meaning: Boar's Head

Origin: This tribe lived in the area between Lakes Huron and Ontario
and called themselves the *Wyandot*, meaning "Those from the Peninsula."
But the French called them *Hures*, or "Boar's Head," because the men in

the tribe wore their hair in bristly spikes that resembled boar's hair—and *Hures* eventually became *Huron*.

WINNEBAGO

Meaning: Filthy Water People

Origin: These Great Lakes Indians were named by the *Chippewa* people. Their own name was *Horogióthe*, or "Fish-Eaters." But the Chippewa called them the *Winnebago*—the "Filthy Water People," possibly because the Horogióthe painted themselves with clay when going to war, which made them appear to have bathed in muddy water.

MOHAWK

Meaning: Man-Eaters

Origin: This tribe from upper New York State and eastern Canada called themselves *Kaniengehagaóthe*, or "Flint People." That proved to be a very difficult word to pronounce for Europeans, who called them what their neighbors, the Narragansett, called them: *Mohawk*, or "Man-Eaters." Why? They engaged in ritualistic cannibalism.

GROS VENTRES

Meaning: Big Bellies

Origin: This tribe from what is now Montana and Saskatchewan called themselves the *Ahahninin*, or "White Clay People." When early French fur trappers and traders asked members of neighboring tribes about the name, they responded—in Native American sign language—by sweeping their hand out from their chest and downward, making what appeared to be a "belly" shape. What were they saying? Historians believe they were saying "Waterfall People," referring to the part of the Saskatchewan River where they lived. The French mistook the gesture and called them the name they are still called today, the *Gros Ventres*—"Big Bellies."

*   *   *

"Names are not always what they seem. The common Welsh name Bzjxxllwcp is pronounced Jackson."

—**Mark Twain**

Even Transylvania? Garlic is used by almost every culture and country in the world.

TRUE COLORS

*Here's something to think about next time you open a box of crayons.
We take it for granted that the pigments used are clean and safe—but as these
colors of the past reveal, that's not necessarily so.*

Color: Mummy Brown

Made From: Actual mummies

How Did That Become a Thing? Long before there were art stores, the most reliable source of powdered chemicals of all kinds was the apothecary. Europeans had gotten it into their heads that Egyptian mummies were powerful medicine, and from the 1300s to the early 20th century, ground mummies were prescribed for everything from headaches to gout to epilepsy. Adventurous artists discovered that when mixed with oil paint, powdered flesh from mummies made an excellent light brown color. It was used extensively from the 1700s into the mid-1920s.

True Colors: Despite the belief that mummies were indestructible, it turned out that flesh in paint tended to shrink and crack with time. But the thing that really doomed Mummy Brown was the dwindling supply of mummies. By 1964, it was officially as dead as a pharaoh; an article in Time magazine quoted a representative of a major art supply house as saying, "We may still have a few limbs lying around somewhere, but not enough to make any more paint."

Color: Royal Purple

Made From: Sea snails

How Did That Become a Thing? When Cleopatra became fond of a very expensive purple dye, she started a long tradition. The color was expensive because making it was difficult and unpleasant. You started by crushing the mucus out of 250,000 sea snails (known as the spiny dye murex) and soaking it for weeks in stale urine. Worse, a quarter million snails could make only half an ounce of dye—enough to color a single toga, a piece of tapestry, or a ceremonial flag or two. The stench was so bad that dyers were required to do their work far outside the city walls. The nauseating smell clung to them even after washing; in fact, the Talmud granted an automatic divorce to women whose husbands became dyers. Yet all that trouble and expense—and even the smell—only made it more attractive to those who wanted to show off their money and power.

True Colors: You'd think that overharvesting of that sea snail would kill the dye. It didn't. Neither did the horrible stench that clung to the fabric. The hue remained a status symbol worn by the royal and the wealthy for many centuries. And it might still be stinking up the place if an 18-year-old chemist named William Perkin hadn't accidentally invented the first synthetic dye in 1856. The color of Perkin's dye was a rich purple he called "mauve." It was also inexpensive, which made it accessible to almost anybody…and that's what killed Royal Purple.

Color: Emerald Green/Paris Green
Active Ingredient: Arsenic
How Did That Become a Thing? Until 1775, green paint was commonly made from copper carbonate—the green rust you see on copper building trim and the Statue of Liberty. That year Carl Scheele, the brilliant Swedish chemist who discovered chlorine, invented a beautifully bright green pigment from an arsenic compound. He called it Scheele's Green, and it quickly replaced the older paints. Unfortunately, nobody was yet aware of how poisonous arsenic was, and Scheele—who had a habit of sniffing and tasting his discoveries—succumbed to heavy metal poisoning from exposure to arsenic, mercury, lead, and other chemicals, and he died in 1786. In 1814 a slightly improved version of his recipe became commercially available as Paris Green or Emerald Green. These arsenic-based pigments became popular among artists and manufacturers of cloths, candles, wallpaper, printing ink, and even candies. Of course, in the 1800s, sudden unexplained deaths weren't unusual, so the Paris Green deaths weren't immediately recognized. Especially dangerous was its use in wall paint and wallpaper: when moisture degraded the pigment, it released deadly arsine gas. (Napoleon, who died in a bright green room with mildew on the walls, was found to have an unusually high amount of arsenic in his hair and bones.)

True Colors: In the 1890s, Italian authorities became aware of a disturbing trend: more than 1,000 apparently healthy children had died mysteriously in recent years. A chemist investigated their homes and discovered that virtually all of them played in rooms with mildew and Emerald Green wallpaper. Arsine gas, heavier than air, tended to stay close to the floor, where kids sat and played. Countrywide removal of the green wallpaper prevented further deaths.

Pop science quiz: Why does peanut butter stick to the roof of your mouth?…

LITTLE WILLIE

These morbid "Willie" poems were popular in the 1950s, although most were written in the 1890s. Either way, they're still funny (in a sick sort of way).

Little Willie hung his sister,
She was dead before
we missed her.
Willie's always up to tricks!
Ain't he cute? He's only six!

Willie poisoned Father's tea.
Father died in agony.
Mother was extremely vexed.
"Really, Will," she
said, "What next?"

Into the family drinking well
Willie pushed his sister Nell.
She's there yet
because it kilt her.
Now we have to buy a filter.

Little Willie, on the track,
Didn't hear the engine squeal.
Now the engine's
coming back,
Scraping Willie off the wheel.

The ice upon our
pond's so thin
That Little Willie's fallen in!
We cannot reach
him from the shore
Until the surface freezes more.
Ah me, my heart
grows weary waiting—
Besides, I want
to do some skating.

Willie saw some dynamite,
Couldn't understand it quite;
Curiosity never pays:
It rained Willie seven days.

Willie with a thirst for gore
Nailed his sister to the door.
Mother said with
humor quaint,
"Willie dear, don't
scratch the paint."

Little Willie fell down a drain;
Couldn't scramble out again.
Now he's floating in the sewer
The world is left
one Willie fewer.

Willie, in one of
his nice new sashes,
Fell in the fire and
was burnt to ashes.
Now, although the
room grows chilly,
We haven't the heart
to poke poor Willie.

Willie coming
home from school,
Spied a dollar near a mule.
Stooped to get it,
quiet as a mouse.
Funeral tomorrow
at Willie's house.

...A: Its high protein content sucks away moisture.

THE MISSING MOM

*Here's a nightmare: You set off on a simple trip, only to end
up more than 1,000 miles away from everyone you've ever
known, with no way to get home. It happened to a
woman who became known as "Auntie Mon."*

LANGUAGE BARRIER

In 1982 Jaeyaena Beuraheng left her home in the Narathiwat Province of southern Thailand to take one of her regular shopping trips across the border in Malaysia. After she was done at the markets, Beuraheng, 51 years old and a mother of seven, accidentally boarded the wrong bus. She fell asleep. When she woke up, she found herself in Bangkok…700 miles north of her home. Unfortunately for Beuraheng, she couldn't speak Thai, and her Malay dialect, Yawi, is spoken by very few people in Bangkok. In fact, to the people in Bangkok whom she asked for directions, it sounded like the woman was speaking gibberish. Without the ability to read signs or ask directions, Beuraheng boarded another bus—one that she thought was headed south. Instead, it took her another 430 miles north and she ended up in the city of Chiang Mai. Beuraheng was now more than 1,100 miles from home, she didn't know where she was, and she'd run out of money.

Meanwhile, back in her hometown, Beuraheng's family told the authorities that their mother was missing and were informed that a woman matching her description had been hit by a train and killed. Beuraheng's son went to identify the body—which was difficult—but he said that it could have been her. So, believing their mother was dead, they stopped searching for her. Beuraheng was on her own. With no other options, she resorted to begging in the street to survive.

A SHELTERED LIFE

Five years later, Beuraheng, now 56, was arrested in a section of the city where begging was not allowed. The police couldn't understand the woman's words, so they took her to a homeless shelter in nearby Phitsanulok. The staff at the shelter deduced that the woman was insane. Still, she seemed nice, so there she stayed. Mostly, Beuraheng sat in a chair and sang a song that no one could understand. They called her "Auntie Mon" because the song reminded them of the language spoken by the ethnic Mon people, who live on the Burma-Thailand border. They even brought in someone who could speak Mon to try and discern if that's what it was, but it wasn't. Everyone who tried to understand Auntie Mon only heard gibberish.

Twenty years passed.

THE POWER OF SONG

In 2007 three university students from Narathiwat were studying the homeless problem in Phitsanulok. As they were touring the shelter, one of the students asked about the old woman singing the song. "That's Auntie Mon. We can't understand her words, but we like the song," said one of the staff workers. The student replied that he could—it was Yawi, a dialect spoken near his hometown. He approached her, smiled, and asked her for her name. It was the first time Beuraheng had understood anything that anyone had said in 25 years. Overjoyed, she told the students about her ordeal—how she took the wrong bus, how she ended up at the shelter, how much she missed being able to speak to anyone, and how much she missed her family.

HOME AT LAST

Beuraheng's family was shocked to receive the news that their mother was alive. Her youngest son and eldest daughter traveled to the shelter to bring her home. She recognized her daughter, but not her son, who was just a small child when she last saw him. They flew back to Narathiwat...and took the *correct* bus home to their village. A two-day celebration ensued, during which Beuraheng—often crying tears of joy—told her amazing story to the press. "I didn't tell anybody where I was going on that day, because I went there quite often. I thought I would die in Phitsanulok. I thought about running away many times, but then I worried I would not be able to make it home. I really missed my children."

Beuraheng, now 79 years old, has a much larger family than when she left (there are many grandchildren). As in the shelter, she still spends much of her time sitting in her chair and singing her song. Only now, those around her can understand the words.

Elvis Presley collected guns, including several M-16s and a Thompson submachine gun.

"GOING, GOING...GONE!"

You've paid your dues at broadcasting school and have finally worked your way up to becoming a play-by-play announcer in the majors. Congratulations! Now all you need is your own signature home run call. (Just don't use any of these—they're already taken.)

"Holy Cow!"
—Phil Rizzuto, Yankees

"Whoa, boy! Next time around, bring me back my stomach!"
—Jack Brickhouse, White Sox

"Tell it 'Bye-Bye, baby!'"
—Russ Hodges, Giants

"Forget it!"
—Vin Scully, Dodgers

"Going back...at the track, at the wall...SSSEEEEE-YA!"
—Michael Kay, Yankees

"Get up, get outta here, gone!"
—Bob Uecker, Brewers

"It's deep, and I don't think it's playable."
—Keith Olbermann, ESPN

"They usually show movies on a flight like that."
—Ken Coleman, Indians, Red Sox, and Reds

"It's going, going...gone!"
—Harry Hartman, Reds (he coined it in 1929)

"Kiss it goodbye!"
—Bob Prince, Pirates

"Long drive, way back, warning track, wall...you can touch 'em all!"
—Greg Schulte, Diamondbacks

"That ball is going and it ain't coming back!"
—Jeff Kingery, Rockies

"To the wall and over the wall! Oh, Doctor!"
—Jerry Coleman, Yankees, Angels, Padres

"Open the window, Aunt Minnie, here it comes!"
—Rosey Roswell, Pirates

"*Bonsoir, elle est partie!*" (French for "So long, she's gone!")
—Rodger Brulotte, Expos

Poo news: Deer droppings are called *fumet*.

FRUITY GEOGRAPHY

*We've treated you to a lot of food name origins over the years.
Here are a few we missed—of the fruity variety.*

PEACH. The English word peach is, surprisingly enough, derived from an ancient Greek name for Persia. The Greeks called the peach the Persikon malon, meaning "Persian apple," or simply Persikos. Reason: It was the Persians who first introduced the fruit—which actually originated in China—to Europe. The Greek name evolved over the centuries, becoming pesca in Latin, and then pesche in Old French, before arriving in English as peach around 1400.

ANJOU PEAR. These creamy pears, sometimes called beurré d'Anjou, meaning "butter of Anjou" in French, are named after the northwest French province of Anjou. But this is believed to be a mistake. Botanists say Anjou pears were bred from the European pear (from which the world's most popular pear cultivars were derived) in the early 1800s, probably in Belgium. When they were first exported to the U.K. and the U.S. in the 1840s, someone named them Anjou—and nobody knows quite why...but that's what they've been called ever since.

FUJI APPLE. In the late 1930s, botanists at the Tohoku Research Station in Fujisaki, Japan, began work on creating an apple that was sweet, crisp, and didn't spoil quickly. It took more than 20 years, but in 1962, the TRS's Fuji apple—as in "Fujisaki"—went to market worldwide. A cross of two American varieties, the Ralls-Genet and the Red Delicious, Fuji apples are very sweet, extra crisp, and are notable for yellow, green, orange, and red stripes. The Fuji is one of the top 10 best-selling apple varieties in the U.S....but it's still the #1 seller in Japan.

CURRANT. This raisin variety got its name from the Greek city of Corinth. In the 13th century, raisins from the Mediterranean region started becoming popular in England. In the 14th century, a special kind of raisin made from very small seedless grapes started selling under the name reisin de Corauntz, meaning "raisin of Corinth," after the city in southern Greece, where these raisins were produced. By 1500, reisin had been dropped, and Corauntz had evolved into currant—still our name for the tiny raisin today. (Extra fact: Currant is also the name of a genus of berries, including the black currant, red currant, and white currant. The berry got that name in the late 1500s—because it resembled the grape-derived currant.)

The word "grandmother" appears in the Bible only once: 2 Timothy 1:5.

UNDERWORLD LINGO

Every profession has its own jargon—even the criminal world. These terms were compiled by someone else. We stole them fair and square... and we're not giving them back, and no copper's gonna make us!

Walk the plank. Appear in a police lineup.

Barber a joint. Rob a bedroom while the occupant is asleep.

Chop a hoosier. Stop someone from betting because they've been continuously winning.

Dingoes. Vagrants who refuse to work even though they claim to be looking for a job.

California blankets. Newspapers used to sleep on or under.

Wise money. Money to be wagered on a sure thing.

Ride the lightning. Be electrocuted.

Rolling orphan. Stolen vehicle with no license plates.

Put [someone] in the garden. Swindle someone out of their fair share of money or property.

Swallow the sours. Hide counterfeit money from the police.

Frozen blood. Rubies.

Square the beef. Get off with a lighter sentence than expected.

Toadskin. Paper money—either good or counterfeit.

Vinegar boy. Someone who passes worthless checks.

Trojan. A professional gambler.

White soup. Stolen silver melted down so it won't be discovered.

Grease one's duke. Put money into someone's hand.

Irish favorites. Emeralds.

Fairy grapes. Pearls.

High pillow. The top man in an organization.

Nest with a hen on. Promising prospect for a robbery.

Trigging the jigger. Placing a piece of paper (the trig) in the keyhole of a door to a house that is suspected to be uninhabited. If the trig is still there the next day, a gang can rob the house later that night.

In Flowery Branch, Georgia, it is illegal to yell "Snake!" within city limits.

CARD-PLAYING SUPERSTITIONS

Over the centuries, card players have come up with all sorts of strange superstitions to help them win—and elaborate explanations for why they're losing. (Ignoring, of course, the possibility that they're just bad card players.)

GOOD LUCK

• Blow on the cards or spit on them, preferably when no one is looking. (Remember to wipe up any excess spit, so no one knows you've fouled them.)

• Wear an article of dirty clothing when you play cards, especially when you play poker. The dirt helps keep evil at bay.

• Stick a pin in your lapel, or in a friend's lapel.

• There's one lucky card in each deck. If you can figure out which card it is, touch it with your index finger before the game begins.

• If you're sitting at a table made of wood, choose a seat that lets you lay your cards with the grain instead of against it.

• Whenever you're on a losing streak, tilt your chair up on its forelegs and twist it three times. This works best if you twist following the path of the sun—i.e., from east to west.

• If twisting doesn't help, rotate the chair so the back faces the table, then sit astride it so that you're facing the seat back.

• If you're sitting astride your chair and still losing, try sitting on a handkerchief, or walk clockwise three times around the table. (If you still lose, switch to a new deck of cards or consider taking up dominos.)

• If you see a hunchback on the way to your game, that's good luck. Don't touch the hump—just seeing the hunchback is all it takes.

BAD LUCK

• Don't sing or whistle during a card game. It's unlucky (not to mention annoying).

---

tudents built a computer out of Tinker Toys. It plays Tic-Tac-Toe. (It's never lost a game.)

• Don't pick up any of your cards until all the cards have been dealt, and when you do pick them up, use your right hand.

• Never, ever let someone hover over you and look at your cards, unless that person never plays cards. If they never play cards, then standing over you may actually bring you luck. People who bring you luck are known as "mascots."

• Don't sit with your legs crossed—it "crosses out your luck."

• Never play cards in a room with a dog in it.

• Never let anyone place their foot on the rung of your chair. On the other hand, if you want to give bad luck to someone who's beating you, put your foot on the rung of *their* chair.

• Never play cards with a cross-eyed man or woman. (This superstition dates back to the days when people thought that cross-eyed people could see the cards of the people sitting next to them.)

MORE BAD LUCK

• Never play cards on a bare table. (Bring felt or a tablecloth, preferably green, with you... just in case.)

• Don't lend money during a card game. Don't borrow it, either.

• If you are dealt a steady succession of black cards, it means that you or someone in your family will die soon.

• If you're a pilot, coal miner, soldier, fisherman, or sailor, you should never carry playing cards on your person. If you do and bad luck occurs—a storm or an enemy attack, for example—throw the cards as far away from you as you can to get rid of the bad luck.

LUCKY AND UNLUCKY CARDS

• The four of clubs is "the devil's bedstead." Discard it unless you absolutely need it. If you're dealt the four of clubs in the first hand of the game, throw down the cards and leave the game—you'll have nothing but bad luck.

• Dropping any card on the floor is bad luck, but dropping one of the black aces is worst of all. If you drop a black ace, leave the game immediately. Nobody recovers from luck that bad.

Barely known fact: "Naked" means to be unprotected; "nude" means unclothed.

SNAP, CRACKLE...FLOP!

*For every successful cereal like Frosted Flakes or Wheaties, there are
hundreds of bombs like Banana Wackies and Ooboperoos.
Here are a few legendary cereal flops.*

Kellogg's Kream Crunch (1963). Frosted-oat loops mixed with
cubes of freeze-dried vanilla-orange or strawberry ice cream.
According to a Kellogg's exec: "The product kind of melted into
gooey ice cream in milk. It just wasn't appetizing."

Sugar Smiles (1953). General Mills' first try at sugar cereal. A bizarre
mixture of plain Wheaties and sugar-frosted Kix. Slogan: "You can't help
smiling the minute you taste it."

Dinos (early 1990s). After the success of Fruity Pebbles, Post tried naming a cereal after the Flintstones' pet dinosaur. "A question that came up
constantly," recalls a Post art director, "was 'We've got Cocoa Pebbles
and Fruity Pebbles...so what flavor is Dino?'...It sounds like something
Fred would be getting off his lawn instead of something you'd want to be
eating."

Day-O (late 1960s). "The world's first calypso-inspired presweetened
cereal," from General Mills.

Ooops (early 1970s). General Mills had so many bombs, they came up
with a cereal they actually *said* was based on a mistake—jingle: "Ooops,
it's a crazy mistake, Ooops, it's a cereal that's great!"

Kellogg's Corn Crackos (1967). The box featured the Waker Upper
Bird perched on a bowl of candy-coated twists. An internal company
memo said: "It looks like a bird eating worms; who wants worms for
breakfast?"

Punch Crunch (1975). A spinoff of Cap'n Crunch. The screaming pink
box featured Harry S., an exuberant hippo in a sailor suit, making goo-
goo eyes at Cap'n Crunch. Many chain stores perceived the hippo as gay
and refused to carry the cereal. Marveled one Quaker salesman: "How
that one ever got through, I'll never understand."

SIX FAMOUS ILLEGITIMATE KIDS

The fascinating stories of six people who were born in situations deemed less than ideal…and made it to the top anyway.

WHO'S YOUR DADDY?

For a long time—until very recently, in fact—children born out of wedlock were treated as second-class citizens, both socially and legally. England's Statute of Merton (1235), for example, stated, "He is a bastard that is born before the marriage of his parents" and prohibited these "illegitimate" children from inheriting the estates of their birth parents. Such laws were common throughout the world for centuries. Amazingly, they weren't fully overturned in the UK until 1969—and not in the United States until 1977. But throughout the ages, there are examples of kids who overcame the odds stacked so unfairly against them—and achieved greatness. Here are a few famous ones.

WILLIAM THE CONQUEROR

Born around 1028 to Robert I, Duke of Normandy (a region of northern France) and his mistress, a young peasant woman known only as Herleva. William was lucky, though—he was raised by his father. (His mother married one of Robert's friends.) When William was named Duke of Normandy upon Robert's death in 1035, a contingent of Norman barons objected. They believed "William the Bastard," as they called him, should have been ineligible. A power struggle ensued, and William eventually came out on top. In 1066 he cemented his place in history when he led Norman forces to defeat the English at the Battle of Hastings and became King William I of England, a seat he held until his death in 1087. With a few exceptions, every British monarch since then is a descendant of "William the Bastard."

ALEXANDER HAMILTON

Born on the British Caribbean island of Nevis sometime around 1755, the second son of Scottish businessman James Hamilton and Rachel

Faucette Buck, an island woman of French descent—who was married to another man. (She would divorce that husband a few years later.) Because his parents weren't married, Alexander wasn't allowed to go to school, so he received private tutoring and taught himself by reading anything he could get his hands on. James abandoned the family in 1765; Rachel died in 1768. Around 1771 Alexander and his brother, James Jr., were adopted by a cousin, but he committed suicide a year later. The boys were then split up, and Alexander came under the care of a merchant named Thomas Stevens. The following year, he was sent to the American colonies, where he attended schools in New Jersey and New York. In 1774 he published his first political writings, in 1775 he joined the New York militia, in 1776 he joined General George Washington's staff, in 1789 President George Washington named him the first U.S. Secretary of the Treasury, and today the face of Alexander Hamilton, a seemingly luckless kid from the West Indies, can be seen on millions of American $10 bills.

SOPHIA LOREN

Appropriately enough, Loren's story sounds like something from a Hollywood movie. She was born Sofia Scicolone in 1934 in a ward for unwed mothers in Rome, Italy. Her mother was Romilda Villani, a 20-year-old piano teacher. Her father, 36-year-old Riccardo Scicolone, was married to someone else and refused to help raise Sofia, although he did grant her the use of his last name. (He did not do the same when he and Villani had a second daughter, Sofia's younger sister Anna Maria, four years later.) The young family lived with Villani's mother in the slums of Nazi-occupied Naples during World War II, subsisting on meager rations, often close to starvation. Things began to look up in 1948, when 14-year-old Sofia became a finalist in a Naples beauty contest. Her mother encouraged her to model and try out for films—and in less than a decade she was a Hollywood star. She won an Academy Award for Best Actress in 1962 and received an Honorary Oscar in 1991 for being "one of world cinema's greatest treasures." Bonus fact: After she made it big, Loren paid her father a million lire (about $1,500) for the right for her sister to use his last name so that Anna Maria would no longer be considered illegitimate.

The first insane asylum in the U.S. opened in 1773 in Williamsburg, Virginia.

THOMAS EDWARD LAWRENCE

In 1885 Thomas Robert Tighe Chapman, 39, a wealthy Irishman and the married father of four young girls, got his daughters' governess, 24-year-old Sarah Lawrence, pregnant. He eventually left his wife for his young mistress, and they went on to have several more children. One, born in Wales in 1888, was a son named Thomas Edward Lawrence. Why Lawrence and not Chapman? Because Chapman had taken Sarah's last name to hide the fact that he was the already-married Thomas Chapman. The family moved several times over the years, finally settling in Oxford, England, where, while living as Mr. and Mrs. Lawrence, they were able to get their children decent educations. Young Thomas eventually graduated from Jesus College in Oxford, made his way to the Middle East, and became an archaeologist, then a British Army officer, then a prolific writer, and, finally, the man still known around the world as "Lawrence of Arabia." And very few people knew that the "Lawrence" in his name came from his mother…because he was born out of wedlock.

LEONARDO DA VINCI

Born in 1452 in the Italian region of Tuscany to a 25-year-old lawyer named Piero Fruosino di Antonio da Vinci and a poor peasant (possibly a slave) named Caterina. (Her age and last name—if she had one—are unknown.) At that time in Tuscany, illegitimacy was treated differently by different families: the boy could have been left to his impoverished mother. Luckily for Leonardo, his father took him in. He was raised in his father's house and, according to many records, looked after by an uncle or possibly a grandfather. When Leonardo was 14, his genius was already obvious, and his father apprenticed him to a Florentine artist, beginning the career of one of the most influential painters, architects, engineers, inventors, and writers in history.

*   *   *

4 REAL CANDIES FROM AROUND THE WORLD
- Shrimps & Bananas (England)
- Uncle Urnie's Candy Ashes (United States)
- SUPER OSAMA BIN LADEN KULFA BALLS (Pakistan)
- Kitten Tongues (Czech Republic)

How big is the principality of Monaco? 370 acres.

DIED ON THE JOHN

*From the darker wing of Uncle John's Stall of Fame, here are
some people who took their last breaths in the bathroom.
(Someday we'll probably put Uncle John on the list.)*

In 1016, 27-year-old King Edmund II of England was murdered in the
bathroom. An assassin hid behind the primitive toilet and, as Edmund
sat, the murderer stepped out and quickly shoved his sword twice
"into the king's bowels."

• Another English monarch, King George II, died on the toilet in 1760
at the age of 77. He woke up at six that morning, drank some chocolate,
and an hour later went to the bathroom, where he died of a ruptured
aorta.

• Evelyn Waugh, one of the greatest English novelists of the 20th
century (*Brideshead Revisited, The Loved One*) had just returned home
from Easter Mass. In recent years, the 62-year-old had put on a lot of
weight. He also drank a lot, smoked cigars, and rarely exercised. He died
"straining at stool" in the bathroom, April 10, 1966.

• Perhaps the most famous death-by-toilet is Elvis Presley's. A combination of weight gain and too many prescription drugs gave the 42-year-old
singer a heart attack while he was "takin' care of business." (At the time
of his death he was reading a book entitled *The Scientific Search for the
Face of Jesus.*)

• Movie producer Don Simpson (*Top Gun, Flashdance*) died in 1996.
While rumors persisted that he died of a cocaine overdose, the truth was
more humble and embarrassing: He died of a heart attack while going to
the bathroom.

• It's commonly believed that Catherine the Great of Russia died after
being "crushed" by a horse. True? Na-a-a-a-y. On that fateful day in
1796, she suffered a stroke while sitting on the toilet, but died in her bed
several hours later.

Early recipes for beer included mushrooms, bay leaves, butter, and bread crumbs.

STAGECOACH RULES

Stagecoach travel has been glamorized by Hollywood: a handsome hero in an immaculate white shirt and string necktie, and a neatly coiffured heroine swaying gently as the stage races across the prairie. Romantic? Yes. Truthful? No. Stagecoaches didn't race—good drivers averaged 5 mph. And passengers arrived covered with dust and aching from the bone-rattling journey. These rigorous conditions created discord, so at every station, Wells Fargo posted this list.

Stagecoach Riders' Nine Commandments

1. Abstinence from liquor is requested. If you must drink, share your bottle; otherwise you will appear to be selfish and unneighborly.

2. If ladies are present, gentlemen are urged to forego smoking pipes or cigars, as the odor is repugnant to the gentle sex. Chewing tobacco is permitted, but spit with the wind, not against it.

3. Gentlemen must refrain from using rough language in the presence of ladies and children.

4. Buffalo robes are provided for your comfort during cold weather. Hogging robes will not be tolerated and the offender will be made to ride with the driver.

5. Don't snore loudly while sleeping or use your fellow passenger's shoulder for a pillow. He (or she) may not understand and friction may result.

6. Firearms may be kept on your person for use in emergencies. Do not fire them for pleasure or shoot at wild animals as the sound riles the horses.

7. In the event of runaway horses, remain calm. Leaping from the coach in panic will leave you injured, at the mercy of the elements, hostile Indians, and hungry coyotes.

8. Forbidden topics of discussion are stagecoach robberies and Indian uprisings.

9. Gents guilty of unchivalrous behavior toward lady passengers will be put off the stage. It's a long walk back. A word to the wise is sufficient.

The American bison was pictured on a 1901 U.S. dollar. It was nicknamed "the buffalo

NAME THAT TEAM

Once an NFL team is named, who thinks about the names that weren't picked? We do.

CINCINNATI RHINOS. Cincinnati has a large German population, and when the city was awarded a professional football team in 1966, owners almost called it the Rhinos—a play on Germany's Rhine River. After somebody pointed out that rhinos are fat and slow, the owners went with Bengals, the name of a football team that played in Cincinnati in the 1930s.

SEATTLE D. B. COOPERS. A 1975 naming contest for the new Seattle NFL franchise brought in 20,365 entries with 1,741 suggestions. Among them: the Lumberjacks, the Soggies, the Running Salmon, the Washington Georges, the Abominable Snowmen…and the D. B. Coopers, after the mysterious hijacker who jumped out of a plane over Washington in 1971. The winning name, submitted by 150 people: the Seahawks (a rarely used nickname for the osprey).

ATLANTA DOGS. In 1965 the NFL awarded Atlanta its first pro sports franchise. But the new team had competition in the popular football programs at Georgia Tech and the University of Georgia. To lure fans from both groups, the owners considered combining Tech's Yellow Jackets with UGA's Bulldogs, and naming the team the Yellow Dogs. Bonus: "Yellow Dog" was also a term for anti-Union Southern Democrats after the Civil War. The owners ultimately decided to have a fan vote, and Falcons won out.

DALLAS STEERS. The Dallas NFL expansion team was all set to begin the 1960 season as the Steers…until owner Tex Schramm realized that his team might be mocked if their mascot was the steer—a castrated male cow raised to be turned into beef. He liked the name "Rangers" but didn't want to be confused with the then-minor league Texas Rangers baseball team. He finally decided on Cowboys.

OAKLAND SEÑORS. In 1960 the *Oakland Tribune* held a name-the-team contest, and the winner was…the Señors. It's likely that the contest was fixed, as a joke—the team's co-owner, real estate developer and local celebrity Chet Soda, called everyone he met "señor." About a week after the name was announced, owners went with the third-place voter getter: the Raiders.

Over a lifetime, the average driver releases 900 pints of gas inside their car.

MADISON AVENUE MUTTS

From beer to burritos, these dogs mean business.

NIPPER, THE RCA DOG

Nipper, a fox terrier, was born in England in 1884 and got his name because he liked to bite visitors on their legs. His original owner was Mark Barroud, brother of English painter Francis Barroud. When Mark died, Francis inherited the dog. According to legend, when a recording of Mark's voice was played at his funeral, Nipper recognized it and stood on Mark's coffin, looking into the horn of the phonograph. Francis Barroud later painted the scene in a work titled *His Master's Voice*.

Around 1900, the Victor Talking Machine Company started using the painting as its logo. Then, in 1928, Nipper (minus the coffin) became the symbol of the Radio Corporation of America when Victor's American rights were sold to RCA.

SPUDS MCKENZIE

"Some guy in our Chicago agency drew a rough sketch of a dog called the Party Animal, for a Bud Light poster," Anheuser-Busch's marketing director told *Sports Illustrated*. "So we had to find a real dog that looked like this drawing." The company picked Honey Tree Evil Eye, a female English bull terrier from Illinois. The poster was supposed to be distributed only to college students, but the beer company's spokesdog was such a hit that the ads started showing up everywhere.

After Spuds made her TV debut during the 1987 Super Bowl, Bud Light sales shot up 20 percent. Spuds retired amid controversy sometime later when the group Mothers Against Drunk Driving accused Anheuser-Busch of using the dog to encourage underage drinking. Honey Tree returned home to Illinois, where she lived until her death in 1993. She was 10 years old.

THE TACO BELL CHIHUAHUA

The most famous fast-food character of the 1990s was invented by chance when two advertising executives, Chuck Bennett and Clay Williams, were eating lunch at the Tortilla Grill in Venice, California. "We saw a little Chihuahua run by that appeared to be on a mission," Bennett says. "We both looked at each other and said, 'That would be funny.'"

The men went on to make Gidget—the model Chihuahua used in the ads—an international superstar. The dog spawned toys, bobbleheads, and a renewed interest in the Chihuahua breed. A respected canine thespian in her own right, Gidget also starred in other projects, most notably as Bruiser's mother in the 2003 film *Legally Blonde 2: Red, White, and Blonde*. She died in 2009 at the age of 15.

MCGRUFF THE CRIME DOG
In the late 1970s, the Ad Council—the organization responsible for producing most public-service announcements—made a deal with the U.S. Justice Department to create an ad campaign to discourage crime. Their first task: invent a spokes-character to deliver the message in commercials. Adman Jack Keil began riding with the New York police to get ideas. He remembers:

> We weren't getting anywhere. Then came a day I was flying home from the West Coast. I was trying to think of a slogan—*crunch crime, stomp on crime.* And I was thinking of animal symbols—*growling at crime, roaring at crime.* But which animal? The designated critter had to be trustworthy, honorable, and brave. Then I thought, you can't crunch crime or defeat it altogether, but you can snap at it, nibble at it—*take a bite out of crime.* And the animal that takes a bite is a dog.

A bloodhound was the natural choice for a crime fighter, and the campaign (dog included) debuted in 1980. But Keil still needed a name for his watchdog, so the Ad Council sponsored a nationwide contest to name the dog. Entries included Shure-lock Bones, Sarg-dog, J. Edgar Dog, and Keystone Kop Dog. The winner—McGruff—was submitted by a police officer from New Orleans. Keil supplied the dog's voice in the ads, and passed away in 2017. Steven Parker, a retired law enforcement officer, took over as the official voice of McGruff.

*   *   *

"Scratch a dog, and you'll find a permanent job."

—**Franklin P. Jones**

Koalas have no natural predators.

SUPPOSEDLY SAID

Because quoting what other people say is often like playing a game of "telephone," what ends up in our collective memory often isn't exactly what the speaker said.

TARZAN

He supposedly said: "Me Tarzan, you Jane."

...**But actually:** This line was never uttered in any Tarzan film, nor in the original Edgar Rice Burroughs novel. The quote stems from an interview in which Tarzan actor Johnny Weissmuller made up the line as a comment on the films' simplistic dialogue.

KARL MARX

He supposedly said: "Religion is the opiate of the masses."

...**But actually:** "Religion is the sigh of the oppressed creature, the heart of a heartless world and the soul of soulless conditions. It is the opium of the people," is what Marx really said. The misquote implies that Marx believed religion "drugs" people. The full quote suggests that Marx had a better understanding of why many people flock to religion.

JOHN KERRY

He supposedly said: "Who among us doesn't like NASCAR?"

...**But actually:** This quote was well circulated during the 2004 presidential election, often characterizing Senator Kerry as awkward, out of touch, and pandering to blue-collar voters. Turns out that when *New York Times* columnist Maureen Dowd mocked Kerry for the quote in a March 2004 column, it was the first time the quote had ever appeared. Dowd had just made it up.

SGT. JOE FRIDAY (Jack Webb)

He supposedly said: "Just the facts, ma'am."

...**But actually:** The no-nonsense cop said, "All we want are the facts, ma'am." Satirist Stan Freberg spoofed he show on the 1953 hit record "St. George and the Dragonet," in which he says, "I just want to get the facts, ma'am." It was Freberg's line, not Webb's, that became synonymous with the show.

Sally Field was voted class clown by her high school classmates.

MARIE ANTOINETTE

She supposedly said: "Let them eat cake."

...But actually: The queen was said to have made this glib remark when told that many people in France had no bread to eat. In reality, French revolutionaries spread the rumor to stir up hatred for the monarch and support for overthrowing the crown.

ADM. DAVID FARRAGUT

He supposedly said: "Damn the torpedoes! Full speed ahead!"

...But actually: According to *The Yale Book of Quotations*, the Civil War admiral never uttered this famous rallying cry at the Battle of Mobile Bay in 1864. It appeared in print in 1878, but news reports and accounts of the battle make no mention of the phrase.

JAMES CAGNEY

He supposedly said: "You dirty rat!"

...But actually: It's commonly assumed to be a line from Cagney's film *Public Enemy Number One*, but the line isn't in that movie...nor in any others. Where the misquote originated is unknown.

THE KING JAMES BIBLE

It supposedly said: "Money is the root of all evil."

...But actually: Money is not evil; loving it is. The full quote is: "For the love of money is the root of all evil" (1 Timothy 6-7).

LORD ACTON

He supposedly said: "Power corrupts. Absolute power corrupts absolutely."

...But actually: The 19th-century British historian really wrote, "Power tends to corrupt. Absolute power corrupts absolutely. Great men are almost always bad men."

WILLIAM CONGREVE

He supposedly said: "Hell hath no fury like a woman scorned."

...But actually: Close, but not quite. In his 1697 poem "The Mourning Bride," Congreve wrote: "Heaven has no rage like love to hatred turned/ Nor hell a fury like a woman scorned."

ars can be found on the thorax, abdomen, legs, wings, and mouths of different insects.

AS HEARD IN CANADA

Canadian slang is much more than "eh," you hoser.

Farmer Vision: The free over-the-air broadcast TV channels available virtually anywhere in Canada

Rink rat: A kid who does chores around a hockey rink in exchange for free skating or admission to hockey games

Chesterfield: In the 1700s, the Earl of Chesterfield commissioned a leather sofa with deep buttons and a low seat. A "chesterfield" now refers to any kind of couch.

Puck bunnies: Hockey groupies

Gonch: There's a sizeable Ukrainian population in British Columbia and Alberta, and a Ukrainian word evolved into a Canadian slang term. The original word is *gatsi*, and it means men's briefs-style underwear. Gotch, ginch, gonch, gitch, ginchies, and gitchies are all derivatives.

Gonch-pull: A wedgie

Gorby: An obnoxious tourist. It comes from the expression "**g**uy **o**n **r**ental **b**oards," coined by employees at Banff ski resorts in the late 1970s.

Vancouver Special: A cheap and easy-to-build suburban home style. They're typically box-shaped, have low ceilings, and have an extra bedroom on the ground floor, often rented out to a tenant—to make ends meet in the expensive city of Vancouver.

Lord Stanley's Mug: The Stanley Cup

TimTart: An attractive female employee of the Tim Hortons doughnut chain

Centre of the Universe: A derisive term for Toronto, used by residents of the rest of Canada (or what Torontonians call "ROC"), referring to the perceived attitude of the citizens of Canada's largest city

Down south: The U.S.

Grocery Police: Many Canadians who live near the U.S. border go "down south" to pick up groceries and consumer goods because they're cheaper there. Upon returning, they have to go through customs and declare what they bought (and pay a tax) to customs officials, or "the grocery police."

In scientific measurement, a unit of beauty is called a *millihelen.*

WHAT IS SPAM?

Everybody's tried it and hardly anyone says they like it…but 30% of all American households have a can on hand. So how much do you know about SPAM? How much do you want to know? Not much, probably. Too bad—we're going to tell you about it anyway.

M AKING A SILK PURSE OUT OF A SOW'S EAR
It's a question as timeless as the pork-packing industry itself: Once you've removed all the choice meat from the carcass of a pig, what do you do with all the pig parts nobody wants?

That's the question the folks at the George A. Hormel Company faced in 1937. Their solution: Take the parts that nobody wants and make them into a loaf nobody wants. Jack Mingo describes the historic moment in his book *How the Cadillac Got Its Fins*:

> Seeing thousands of pounds of pork shoulders piling up in the Hormel coolers in 1937 gave one of the company's executives an idea: Why not chop the meat up, add some spices and meat from other parts of the pig, and form it into small, hamlike loaves? Put it in a can and fill the excess space with gelatin from the pig's leftover skin and bones—you could probably keep the meat edible for months without refrigeration. They tried it. It worked. Hormel's Spiced Ham quickly found a niche in the market. It was inexpensive, savory, and convenient, and it didn't need refrigeration.

PORCINE PLAGIARISM
But pig parts were piling up just as high at other pork packers, and as soon as they saw Hormel's solution they began selling their own pig loafs. Afraid of being lost in the sow shuffle, Hormel offered a $100 prize to anyone who could come up with a brand name that would make its pork product stand out from imitators. The winner: A brother of one of the Hormel employees, who suggested turning "Spiced Ham" into "SPAM."

PIGS AT WAR
Described by one writer as "a pink brick of meat encased in a gelatinous coating," SPAM seems pretty gross to folks who aren't used to it (and

even to plenty who are). It probably wouldn't have become popular if it hadn't been for World War II.

Because it was cheap, portable, and didn't need refrigeration, SPAM was an ideal product to send into battle with U.S. GIs. It became such a common sight in mess halls (where it earned the nickname "the ham that didn't pass its physical") that many GIs swore they'd never eat the stuff again. Even General Dwight Eisenhower complained about too much SPAM in army messes.

THEIR SECRET SHAME

American G.I.s *said* they hated SPAM, but evidence suggests otherwise. Forced to eat canned pork over a period of several years, millions of soldiers developed a taste for it, and when they returned home they brought it with them. SPAM sales shot up in supermarkets after the war.

Laugh if you want (even Hormel calls it "the Rodney Dangerfield of luncheon meat—it don't get no respect"), but SPAM is still immensely popular: 12.8 cans of SPAM are consumed every second, over 400 million cans a year.

SPAM FACTS

• More than eight billion cans of SPAM have been sold around the world since the product was invented in 1937. "Nowhere," says Carolyn Wyman in her book *I'm a SPAM Fan*, "is SPAM more prized than in South Korea, where black-market SPAM regularly flows from U.S. military bases and locally produced knockoffs, such as Lospam, abound. In fact, young Korean men are just as likely to show up at the house of a woman they are courting with a nine-can gift pack of SPAM as wine or chocolate."

• SPAM may have helped defeat Hitler. Nikita Khrushchev, himself a war veteran, credited a U.S. Army shipment of SPAM with keeping Russian troops alive during World War II. "We had lost our most fertile, food-bearing lands," he wrote in *Khruschev Remembers*, "Without SPAM, we wouldn't have been able to feed our army."

• SPAM isn't as gross as legend would have you believe. There aren't any lips, eyes, or other pig nasties in it—just pork shoulder, ham, salt, sugar, and the preservative sodium nitrate.

STATUE RATS

They're called "flying carp," "winged weasels," "scum of the sky,"
"park lice," and "winged infestation." Lawyers? No, pigeons.
They don't get much respect, but maybe they should.
There's more to them than you might think.

• Pigeons were first domesticated by the ancient Egyptians more than 5,000 years ago.

• Pigeons can see clearly for 25 miles and hear wind changes hundreds of miles away.

• Pigeons mate for life and share parenting duties. The father sits on the eggs during the day, the mother at night.

• Pigeons are the only birds that don't have to lift their heads to swallow water.

• Passenger pigeons were once the most numerous birds in the world. Ornithologist John J. Audubon recorded seeing a single flock in 1808 that he calculated to be 150 miles long, numbering over two billion birds. By 1914 hunting and deforestation had led to the total extinction of the birds.

• Ever seen a baby pigeon? You probably have: young pigeons grow extremely fast. They may weigh more than their parents by the time they're only four to six weeks.

• In the 17th century, pigeon droppings were used to tan hides and to make gunpowder.

• Homing pigeons were used in both world wars to carry messages between troops and headquarters. They had a 98% success rate in missions flown.

• Racing pigeons have been clocked at 110 mph.

• Only mammals produce milk, right? Wrong. Pigeons make "pigeon milk," an extremely nutritious secretion from the "crop," a chamber at the bottom of the esophagus. Both parents make it and feed their young with it.

• Racing pigeons are bred for speed. In 1992 champion racer *Invincible Spirit* was sold for over $130,000.

• Why do pigeons live in cities? One theory: They are descended from rock doves, cliff dwellers that live near the Mediterranean. Urban structures mimic those ancestral cliffs.

BIERCE-ISMS

Author and newspaper columnist Ambrose Bierce (1842–1914) often peppered his articles with his own humorous—and cynical—definitions for common words. Here are a few of our favorites.

Dentist: A magician who, putting metal into your mouth, pulls coins out of your pocket.

Positive: Mistaken, at the top of one's voice.

Acquaintance: A person whom we know well enough to borrow from, but not well enough to lend to.

Dog: An additional Deity designed to catch the overflow and surplus of the world's worship.

Clairvoyant: A person who has the power of seeing that which is invisible to her patron—namely, that he is a blockhead.

Revolution: An abrupt change in the form of misgovernment.

Corporation: An ingenious device for obtaining individual profit without individual responsibility.

Admiration: Our polite recognition of another's resemblance to ourselves.

Saint: A dead sinner, revised and edited.

Alliance: The union of two thieves who have their hands so deeply inserted in each other's pockets that they cannot separately plunder a third.

Responsibility: A detachable burden easily shifted to the shoulders of God, Fate, Fortune, Luck, or one's neighbor.

Appeal: In law, to put the dice into the box for another throw.

Coward: One who in a perilous emergency thinks with his legs.

Famous: Conspicuously miserable.

Friendship: A ship big enough to carry two in fair weather, but only one in foul.

Husband: One who, having dined, is charged with the care of the plate.

Meekness: Uncommon patience in planning a revenge that is worthwhile.

Outcome: A particular type of disappointment.

Love: A temporary insanity curable by marriage.

"Always and never are two words you should...

TAKE A HINT

*Whether you call them "everyday shortcuts" or "life hacks," these simple
household tips are bound to make you ask, "Why didn't I think
of that?" (And they're very entertaining.)*

Place a coin inside the bottom hem of a tie to keep it from flying around and smacking you in the face on a windy day.

• Throw wrinkled shirts in the dryer with a few ice cubes for 10 minutes on high to steam away the wrinkles.

• To help remove deodorant stains on your shirt, rub a dryer sheet on the stain before washing it.

• To keep canvas shoes dry in the rain, rub beeswax over them and blow dry until the wax melts. That will create a waterproof seal.

• Cheetos are delicious, but the sticky orange fingers you get after handling them are a pain. Use chopsticks instead to keep your fingers clean.

• Keep pizza hot on the ride home by putting the pizza box on your car seat and turning on the seat warmer.

• Do you bang your fingers with a hammer every time you nail something into a wall? Use a fine-tooth comb to keep the nail in place and keep your fingers safe.

• Scratches in wood can be fixed by rubbing a de-shelled walnut over the area.

• Putting a dry tea bag in your shoes overnight will absorb funky odors. (But remember to throw away the bags when you're done.)

• For an effective way to clean a dirty toilet, drop in a couple of denture tablets. After 20 minutes, scrub the toilet bowl and flush.

• Spraying nonstick cooking spray on shovels will keep them ice-free while you're shoveling snow.

• Price tag stickers are usually a nightmare to remove. Once you've picked away most of the tag, slather peanut butter over the site and wipe with a cloth to remove any remaining glue residue.

• Running a slightly damp rubber glove over furniture will pick up pet hair quickly and easily.

• After sweeping up the remnants of a broken glass, press a slice of bread over the area. Any remaining glass bits will stick to the bread.

BASEBALL'S DISABLED (AND EMBARRASSED) LIST

Uncle John was supposed to have this article done a month ago, but he broke three of the fingers on his typing hand when he jammed them in the toilet paper dispenser. It turns out he's not the only guy to hurt himself in a way that he'd rather not talk about.

Vince Coleman (St. Louis Cardinals, 1985): Bruised his leg and chipped a bone in his knee when a mechanical tarp at Busch Stadium rolled over him while he was stretching before a playoff game. (He wasn't paying attention.) Coleman ended up missing the rest of the postseason, including the World Series, which the Cardinals lost to the Kansas City Royals in seven games. "That tarp was a real maneater," said Coleman.

• **Bill Lee (Montreal Expos, 1979):** While jogging in Montreal, Lee jumped into the street to avoid a cat and was hit by a taxi.

• **Pea Ridge Day (St. Louis Cardinals, 1920s):** Famous for his hog calls and his ability to snap leather belts by expanding his chest, Day broke three ribs while demonstrating the latter.

• **Dwight Gooden (New York Mets, 1990):** Suffered a broken toe when teammate Mackey Sasser placed a metal folding chair on his left foot and sat on it without looking. The incident caused Gooden to miss a game; three years later he missed another game when Vince Coleman hit his shoulder with a nine-iron while practicing his golf swing in the locker room.

• **Marty Cordova (Baltimore Orioles, 2002):** Fell asleep in a tanning bed and suffered burns to his face and other body parts.

• **Eric Show (Oakland A's, 1991):** Stabbed himself in the finger with a toothpick; the resulting infection kept him out for 15 days.

• **Jerry May (Pittsburgh Pirates, 1969):** Crashed into the dugout while trying to make a catch. While being rushed to the hospital for that injury, he injured his shoulder when the ambulance he was riding in got into an accident. *That* injury cost May his job with the Pirates; his career never recovered.

• **Clarence Blethen (Boston Red Sox, 1923):** Blethen, who'd lost all his teeth by the age of 30, liked to intimidate batters by removing his dentures and grimacing when he pitched. During one game, he forgot to put them back in after batting; they were still in his back pocket when he slid into second base. He is the only player in major league history (as far as we know, anyway) to bite himself in the butt during a game.

• **Greg Minton (San Francisco Giants, 1985):** Drove a nail into his pitching hand while trying to shoe a horse.

• **Wade Boggs (Boston Red Sox, mid-1980s):** Sprained his back after he lost his balance while trying to remove his cowboy boots.

• **Steve Sparks (Milwaukee Brewers, 1994):** Pitcher Sparks dislocated his shoulder while trying to tear a phone book in half, a stunt demonstrated to him earlier in the week by motivational speakers hired by the team.

• **Jose Cardenal (Chicago Cubs, 1972):** Missed a game due to exhaustion when crickets in his hotel room kept him up all night.

• **Randy Veres (Florida Marlins, 1995):** Another hotel-related injury: Veres injured the tendon in his right pinkie while punching his headboard several times when the people in the next room wouldn't quiet down.

• **Bret Barberie (Florida Marlins, 1995):** Missed a game after he was "blinded" by his chili-pepper nachos—he failed to wash his hands thoroughly before putting in his contact lenses.

• **David Wells (San Diego Padres, 2004):** Kicked a 40-lb. iron bar stool, lost his balance, and fell on a beer glass, cutting his left hand and a tendon in his right wrist.

• **Glenallen Hill (Toronto Blue Jays, 1990):** A sleepwalker who's also terrified of spiders, Hill suffered cuts and bruises on his hands, feet, and elbow after he smashed his foot through a glass coffee table and fell down a flight of stairs while "fleeing" the spiders in one of his dreams. The incident landed him on the 15-day disabled list and earned him the nickname "Spiderman."

largest ant colony in the world is in Southern Europe—it stretches for over 3,700 miles.

THE COST OF WAR

Whether you're a history buff or just someone who keeps up with current events, you've probably wondered how the cost of the wars in Iraq and Afghanistan compare to, say, the Vietnam War. Or how the cost of the Civil War compares to World War I or World War II. Here are some estimates taken from official U.S. government reports.

Revolutionary War (1775–83)
Cost at the time: $101 million
In 2011 dollars: $2.4 billion

The War of 1812 (1812–15)
Cost at the time: $90 million
In 2011 dollars: $1.55 billion

The Mexican War (1846–48)
Cost at the time: $71 million
In 2011 dollars: $2.37 billion

Civil War, Union (1861–65)
Cost at the time: $3.1 billion
In 2011 dollars: $59.6 billion

Civil War, Confederacy
Cost at the time: $1 billion
In 2011 dollars: $20.1 billion

The Spanish American War (1898)
Cost at the time: $283 million
In 2011 dollars: $9 billion

World War I (1917–1919)
Cost at the time: $20 billion
In 2011 dollars: $334 billion

World War II (1941–45)
Cost at the time: $296 billion
In 2011 dollars: $4.1 trillion

The Korean War (1950–53)
Cost at the time: $30 billion
In 2011 dollars: $341 billion

The Vietnam War (1965–75)
Cost at the time: $111 billion
In 2011 dollars: $738 billion

Persian Gulf War (1990–91)
Cost at the time: $61 billion
In 2011 dollars: $102 billion

Afghanistan War (2001–12)
Cost in 2012 dollars: $823 billion

Iraq War (2003–2012)
Cost in 2012 dollars: $557 billion

Note: Estimates include military operations only. They do not include veterans' benefits, interest on war-related debt, aid to allies, etc.

That spot on your back that you can't scratch is called the *acnestis.*

LOCAL HEROES

*Here are the stories of ordinary people who were
faced with an extraordinary situation…
and did something about it.*

SPILT MILK
Local Hero: Steve Leech, a milkman in Cornwall, England
Heroic Deed: Putting out a dangerous fire

The Story: Leech was making his regular deliveries one morning when he noticed smoke pouring out of a gift shop along his route. He called 999 (the English equivalent of 911) but then decided not to wait for the fire fighters to arrive. "I saw the row of apartments up above the shop," he explains, "and I thought, bloody hell, I'd better do something!"

What did Leech do? He kicked open the door of the shop and started pouring milk on the fire. By the time the firefighters arrived 15 minutes later, the fire was under control—and Leech is credited with saving the row of eight shops, as well as the lives of the people living in the apartments above them. "It was hard work opening all those bottles, since they have tamper-proof lids," he says, "but it was even harder trying to explain to my boss where all the milk (320 pints) had gone."

Update: Leech needn't have worried about his boss—he not only kept his job, in January 2002 England's National Dairymen's Association named him the "Hero Milkman of the Millennium."

FIRST-RATE THIRD GRADER
Local Hero: Austin Rosedale, a third-grader at Sunny Hills Elementary School in Issaquah, Washington
Heroic Deed: Saving his teacher from choking

The Story: Austin was in the computer lab one day in November 2001 when his teacher, Mrs. Precht, started choking on a cough drop. She was just about to pass out when he sprang into action.

Luckily for Precht, Austin's parents had given him a Day Planner organizer that happened to have an instructional diagram of the Heimlich maneuver printed on the cover. Austin had read it so many times that helping Mrs. Precht was a snap. With two thrusts to her abdomen, he dislodged the cough drop. "I just visualized the pictures," he says, "and remembered what I'd read."

BLUE'S BROTHER

Local Hero: Art Aylesworth, a Montana insurance agent

Heroic Deed: Helping to save the mountain bluebird and the western bluebird from extinction

The Story: A longtime conservationist, Aylesworth had worked on a few wildlife habitat restoration projects. But in the mid-1970s he became alarmed when he learned that extensive logging in the state was pushing the bluebirds—which nest in the cavities of old trees—toward extinction. So he got some scrap lumber and built some nest boxes for the birds; then he founded an organization called the Mountain Bluebird Trails Group and recruited hundreds of volunteers to do the same thing.

The organization gave the boxes to anyone willing to put them up and keep an eye on them; it estimates that over the next 25 years, it gave away more than 35,000 boxes. Did it work? Yes—when Aylesworth started handing out the boxes in 1974, only a handful of the bluebirds were thought to still exist; by 1998 the count had grown to more than 17,000.

GUN CONTROL

Local Hero: Dale Rooks, a crossing guard at Suter Elementary School in Pensacola, Florida

Heroic Deed: Finding a unique way to get speeding motorists to slow down in front of the elementary school

The Story: For years Rooks had tried everything he could think of to get drivers to slow down in front of the school—including waving his hands and yelling—but nothing worked. Then inspiration struck him—he got an old hair dryer and covered it with gray duct tape so that it looked like a radar gun, and started pointing it at speeders. That did the trick. "People are slowing down, raising their hands at me apologetically," he says. "It's amazing how well it works."

Update: Inspired by his example, fifth-graders at the school set up a lemonade stand and raised $93 to buy Rooks a *real* radar gun. "I don't mean it to be funny," he says, "but it looks just like a hair dryer."

In Tokyo, the "911" emergency number is 119.

STAR TREK WISDOM

Is there intelligent life in TV's outer space? You decide.

"Is there anyone on this ship who, even remotely, looks like Satan?"
—**Kirk**

Tuvok: "The phaser beam would ricochet along an unpredictable path, possibly impacting our ship in the process."
Janeway: "All right, we won't try that."

"Mr. Spock, the women on your planet are logical. That's the only planet in the galaxy that can make that claim."
—**Kirk**

"I'm a doctor, not an escalator."
—**McCoy**

"I must say, there's nothing like the vacuum of space for preserving a handsome corpse."
—**Doctor**

"It's difficult to work in a group when you're omnipotent."
—**Q**

"The best diplomat I know is a fully-loaded phaser bank."
—**Scotty**

"Mr. Neelix, do you think you could possibly behave a little less like yourself?"
—**Tuvok**

"What am I, a doctor or a moon shuttle conductor?"
—**McCoy**

"Time travel. From my first day on the job I promised myself I'd never let myself get caught up in one of these God-forsaken paradoxes. The future is the past; the past is the future. It all gives me a headache."
—**Janeway**

"I'm attempting to construct a mnemonic memory circuit, using stone knives and bearskins."
—**Spock**

Data: "Tell me, are you using a polymer-based neuro-relay to transmit organic nerve impulses to the central processor of my positronic net?"
Borg Queen: "Do you always talk this much?"

"I'm a doctor, not a bricklayer."
—**McCoy**

WEIRD CANADA

Some great weird news from the Great White North.

GUMMING UP THE COURTS

Elise Pawlow of Edmonton, Alberta, sued Kraft Canada in 2012. Kraft manufactures Stride Gum, whose advertisements claim it is "ridiculously long-lasting." Was Pawlow suing for false advertising, because the gum's flavor gave out after a few minutes? Nope. She sued for $100,000 because the gum worked too well. She claimed that after chewing a single piece of Stride, she had to scrub her dentures to remove tiny specks of the resilient, long-lasting gum, which, she claims, made her extremely depressed for "approximately 10 minutes." (Case dismissed.)

CLASS PRANK

Five teachers at a Windsor, Ontario, middle school announced in early 2013 that the eighth grade's annual class trip would be to Disney World! They told the students in an assembly, and prepared a video and PowerPoint presentation to detail the trip. It was such a happy moment that the teachers made sure to videotape the kids' priceless reactions. They also got their reactions on tape when they informed the kids that it was all a prank—they were really going bowling. When the school principal found out, he came up with a trip that he felt was less expensive than Disney World but more exciting than bowling, and sent the kids to Niagara Falls.

I CAN EXPLAIN!

In January 2013, Richard Blake was on trial in Ottawa, accused of breaking into a home and assaulting two people that lived there. The prosecution had some pretty daunting physical evidence against him, including a knit cap left at the scene of the crime with blood on it that matched Blake's. He was also picked out of a lineup by an eyewitness and the victims. On the witness stand, Blake offered this bizarre explanation for all of it. The reason he had the keys to the victims' car at the time of his arrest was because "a stranger" gave them to him, along with a bloody knife, gloves, and hat, which he put on after he took off his own. And the reason he ran from the scene and hid in a tree, Blake said, was to hide from a swarm of flies. Blake was found guilty of all charges.

SNOW JOB

Since the mid-2000s, Ottawa resident Doug Rochow has done a good deed for his neighborhood, free of charge: Whenever it snows (which can be a lot in Ottawa), he shovels two paths through a city park near his home, providing a safe walking path for local residents. But in March 2013, city officials told Rochow to stop immediately. For while Rochow may have wanted to prevent people from getting injured, the city told him that if the paths were cleared, more people would use them, thus *increasing* the likelihood of injury and, they feared, lawsuits against the city.

POLE POSITION

In 2012, the city of Johnville, Quebec, opened a rebuilt Highway 251—a brand new, two-lane affair. Part of the new road ran through an area where the municipal water company had a utility pole. The water company didn't bother to take down the pole until two months after the highway was open to traffic—meaning that for two months, a large pole sat in the middle of the road. (Amazingly, nobody ran into it.)

BUFFALO GALS

NFL football is extremely popular in southeastern Canada, particularly the nearest "local" team, the Buffalo Bills. In fall 2011, a Kingston, Ontario, radio station announced it was giving away highly sought-after Bills tickets worth $300. All the lucky contestants had to do was find them. The location: They were buried in a kidsized plastic swimming pool filled with buffalo manure. Five contestants dug, live on-air, until DJ Sarah Crosbie was overwhelmed by the odor and vomited. One finalist did get the tickets; the others, even after the tickets were found, kept digging until they found the second-place prize: a pair of tickets to the zoo.

*   *   *

"An optimist is an accordion player with a business card."

—Jay Leno

...were noted abolitionists in the 19th century.

I APOLOGIZE

With our sincerest regrets, we're very sorry to bring you this collection of some of the funniest and strangest apologies ever uttered.

"We apologize for the error in last week's paper in which we stated that Mr. Arnold Dogbody was a defective in the police force. We meant, of course, that Mr. Dogbody is a *detective* in the police farce."

—*Ely Standard* (U.K.)

"My family and I are deeply sorry for all that Vice President Cheney and his family have had to go through this past week."

—**Harry Whittington, Washington lawyer, after Dick Cheney shot *him* in the face**

"In previous issues of this newspaper, we may have given the impression that the people of France were snail swallowing, garlic munching surrender-monkeys whose women never bother to shave their armpits. We now realise that the French football team can stop the Portuguese from getting to the World Cup Final. We apologise profusely to France. *Vive la France!*"

—*Daily Star* (U.K.), **after France beat the U.K.'s rival, Portugal, in the 2006 World Cup semifinals**

"I am so terribly sorry for urinating outside of a public place in your city. It was not a very intelligent thing to do."

—**a man charged with public urination in Fond du Lac, Wisconsin, where all offenders now have to write letters of public apology**

"I'm sorry I bet on baseball."

—**Pete Rose, written on 300 baseballs that he then sold at $1,000 each**

"Oh, goodness, I regret it, it was a mistake! I'm solely responsible for it, and I'm very, very sorry. It was a mistake, I was wrong, it's my fault, and I'm very, very sorry to hurt anyone."

—**Sen. George Allen (R–VA), after referring to an Indian-American constituent as a "macaca"**

"We ate everything but his boots."

—**part of an apology from the Navatusila tribe of Fiji, who killed and ate a British missionary in 1867, to the missionary's descendants**

DEATH CUSTOMS

The treatment and disposal of a dead body is a sacred ritual in every culture, but each one does it a little bit differently.

IN INDIA, custom calls for a body to be burned on a funeral pyre near a riverbank and a temple; the ashes are thrown into the river. Some adherents to Zoroastrianism place bodies atop towers; after the flesh is eaten by vultures, the bones are thrown into a pit at the center of the tower.

IN THE SOLOMON ISLANDS of the South Pacific, a body was traditionally placed on a reef where it would be eaten by sharks.

INUIT PEOPLE constructed small igloos around a corpse (like an "ice tomb"). The cold protected and preserved the body (unless a polar bear found its way in).

THE NAVAJO feared being haunted by the dead, so the body was burned and the deceased's house was destroyed. On the way back from the funeral, relatives took a long, circuitous route to confuse the spirit into not following them.

A VIKING FUNERAL: At sunset, the dead man was placed on a small boat. As it drifted out to sea, it was lit on fire. If the color of the sunset was the same as that of the fire, it meant the deceased was bound for Valhalla (Viking heaven).

MUSLIMS do not use caskets (unless required by law). The body is washed three times, wrapped in a white shroud, and placed directly in the ground with the head pointed toward Mecca.

THE IROQUOIS buried corpses in shallow graves, but exhumed them after a few months. Relatives then placed the bones in a community burial plot.

IN MODERN JAPAN, bodies are washed in a Buddhist temple, dressed (men in suits, women in kimonos), and put in a casket with a white kimono, sandals, and six coins, all for the spirit's crossing into the afterlife. After a funeral, the body is cremated. Relatives pick bones out of the ash, put them in an urn, and bury it.

THE JOY OF SECTS: A QUIZ

And by that, we mean religious sects—particularly the ones that thrive in Pennsylvania. Here's a quiz to help you avoid embarrassing gaffes the next time you're visiting the Keystone State. (Answers on page 196.)

1. You see a group of girls in old-fashioned clothes. They're probably…

A. Mennonites

B. Quakers

C. Amish

D. Moravians

2. One weekend, you notice men moving benches into a home that has dark green window shades. You should…

A. Call the police to report a bizarre case of burglary, in which thieves are putting furniture *into* the house.

B. Check the entertainment guide in the local paper to see if a concert is scheduled.

C. Realize it's basketball season, buy some pretzels and beer, knock on the door, and ask if you can watch the game.

D. Ignore the whole thing, unless you're Amish.

3. You're invited to a "Love Feast" at the local Moravian church. You should…

A. Bring all your souvenir buttons from Woodstock.

B. Practice your musical scales.

C. Bake a pie.

D. Make sure the iPod is charged up because there's likely to be a long, boring sermon.

4. You're at an all-day religious service with non-stop sermons. The preachers don't pause, even when the listeners get up to eat. At the end of it all, people pair off and wash each other's feet. Who are these people?

A. Quakers

B. Amish

C. Schwenkfelders

D. Moravians

5. A Mennonite, a Quaker, an Amish, and a Moravian walk into a bar. Which one orders tea?

Who has the world's largest shell collection? The Smithsonian (over 15 million specimer

RAMBO, STARRING AL PACINO

Some roles are so closely associated with a specific actor that it's hard to imagine he or she wasn't the first choice. But it happens all the time. Can you imagine, for example…

GENE HACKMAN AS HANNIBAL LECTER (*The Silence of the Lambs*, 1991). Hackman wanted to direct the film, star, and write the screenplay, so Orion Pictures bought the rights to the novel. Then Hackman realized how violent the film would be and dropped out. Director Jonathan Demme signed Anthony Hopkins for the part without telling Orion head Mike Medavoy, who was furious that "an Englishman" would play Lecter. Medavoy agreed on one condition: that Jodie Foster be cast as FBI agent Clarice Starling instead of Meg Ryan. Demme agreed; Foster won her second straight Oscar.

GOLDIE HAWN AND MERYL STREEP AS THELMA AND LOUISE (*Thelma and Louise*, 1991). Streep wanted to test her comedic talents; Hawn's film *Private Benjamin* had made $100 million at the box office. They seemed perfect for the film, and wanted to work together. But their schedules were full. "We weren't available right then," Hawn says, "and the director, Ridley Scott, wouldn't wait." Michelle Pfeiffer and Jodie Foster turned down the film; so did Cher. So Scott gave the parts to Geena Davis and Susan Sarandon.

ELVIS PRESLEY AS JOE BUCK (*Midnight Cowboy*, 1969). Desperate to be taken seriously as an actor, the King went shopping around for "a more serious movie role." The part of the male prostitute in *Midnight Cowboy* was one of the parts he considered, but he ultimately turned the film down and did one called *A Change of Habit* instead. Reason: "Since it was about a doctor (Elvis) and a nun (Mary Tyler Moore) in the ghetto, that qualified as being more 'serious.'" *A Change of Habit* was Elvis's biggest box office dud; *Midnight Cowboy* won the Oscar for Best Picture and turned Jon Voight into a star.

er WWI, the German government trained the first guide dogs to assist blind war veterans.

AL PACINO AS RAMBO (*First Blood*, 1982). Pacino wasn't the first major star interested in the part of John Rambo. (Clint Eastwood, Robert De Niro, and Paul Newman turned it down.) He wanted Rambo to be "a little more of a madman," and had the script rewritten. But the new draft made the character too dark and nutty, so Pacino passed on the role. So did John Travolta, Michael Douglas, and Nick Nolte. Then Carolco Pictures bought the script and offered it to Sylvester Stallone, who rewrote the insane Vietnam vet into a misunderstood American hero, "kind of like a Rocky movie." *First Blood* was Stallone's first non-*Rocky* film that didn't bomb. It saved his career. The sequel, *Rambo*, established it for good.

DORIS DAY AS MRS. ROBINSON (*The Graduate*, 1967). Day's Hollywood image was "the perennial virgin." "There was something about taking that All-American housewife image and turning it all around," said producer Larry Turman. "I sent the script to her, but we never heard a thing." Day later explained that she read the script, but just couldn't see herself playing the role. So it was offered to Anne Bancroft, who could.

BURT REYNOLDS AS RANDALL P. McMURPHY (*One Flew Over the Cuckoo's Nest*, 1975). When Marlon Brando turned down the part, director Milos Forman had breakfast with Burt Reynolds and told him he was one of two actors being considered for the part. Reynolds was thrilled. "If the other guy isn't Jack Nicholson," he replied, "I've got the part." When Forman stopped eating dead in his tracks, Reynolds knew he wasn't going to get the part. Nicholson got the role, and won the Oscar for best actor.

BURT REYNOLDS AS GARRETT BREEDLOVE (*Terms of Endearment*, 1983). About 10 years after Reynolds was turned down for *Cuckoo's Nest*, director James L. Brooks sent him the script for *Terms of Endearment*. The lead had been created especially for him, but Reynolds rejected it. "I'd promised that I'd star in *Stroker Ace*," he explained later. So Brooks offered the part to Jack Nicholson, who jumped at it. "How many scripts make you cry?" Nicholson said. "I read hundreds of screenplays every year and this one made me think, 'Yeah, I know just how this guy feels.' It was terrific." *Stroker Ace* was one of the more forgettable films of the year; *Terms of Endearment* won Nicholson his second Oscar.

Storm rule of thumb: If it has wind speeds greater than 74 mph, it's a hurricane.

GENERIC CANADA

A "genericized brand name" is a brand name that has come to be used as the name for that product, whether that particular company made it or not. Examples: Kleenex, Thermos, and Coke. Canada has some that are all its own.

NAME: VI-CO
Refers to: Chocolate milk
Details: The Vi-Co brand of chocolate milk was available in Saskatchewan and Manitoba in the early 20th century. (Vi-Co is short for "vitamins + cocoa.") The last dairy to own the trademark, Dairy Producers, was bought out in 1995 by rival Dairyland, which discontinued the Vi-Co brand. Even though you can't get actual Vi-Co anywhere anymore, many Saskatchewanians still call any kind of packaged chocolate milk "Vi-Co" or "vico."

Name: Kraft Dinner
Refers to: Macaroni and cheese
Details: It's kind of a stereotype now, but Canadians are known for their love of Kraft's blue-boxed Macaroni and Cheese Dinner, or, as it's called, Kraft Dinner. (Worldwide, Canadians purchase a quarter of all the Kraft Dinners sold.) Kraft isn't the only company that packages dry noodles with cheesy sauce, but competitive brands are still more likely to be referred to as "Kraft Dinner" than "macaroni and cheese."

Name: Javex
Refers to: Bleach
Details: Clorox is a genericized trademark in the United States, referring to any bottle of simple bleach, whether or not it's actually Clorox. The same phenomenon occurred in Canada, with Javex. Canada has a strong French influence, and bleach was invented in Javel, a Parisian neighborhood, in the late 1700s. It was first called *eau de Javel* (Javel water), and as Javel gave way to Javex in the early 1900s, it became one of the first bleach brands available in Canada. Javex doesn't exist anymore—the Clorox Corporation bought Javex in 2006 and phased out the name. Canadians now buy Clorox...but they still call it Javex.

17% of sales reps who golf with clients say they let the clients win.

Name: Gravol

Refers to: Anti-motion sickness drugs

Details: If you're feeling seasick or carsick, what remedy do you buy at the pharmacy? Motion sickness pills or Dramamine? In the United States, you'd probably ask for Dramamine. In Canada, the equivalent of Dramamine (and the best known brand name of this kind of drug) is Gravol. Both drugs contain the same active ingredient, dimenhydrinate.

Name: Timbits

Refers to: Doughnut holes

Details: The most popular fast-food restaurant in Canada—by far—is Tim Hortons. It's a coffee-and-doughnut chain founded by ex-professional hockey player Tim Horton in 1964. There are 3,000 locations in Canada, or one for every 12,000 people (by contrast, in the U.S. there's one McDonald's for every 260,000 people). That total market saturation has affected the language. The bite-sized treat made from leftover dough in the doughnut-making process is known at Tim Hortons as a "timbit." Dunkin' Donuts locations in Canada serve doughnut holes (called "munchkins")…but lots of people still order them as "timbits."

Name: Mackinaw

Refers to: A heavy red-and-black-plaid jacket

Details: One Canadian stereotype is the image of a manly lumberjack wearing a thick double-breasted plaid jacket. Lumberjacks did indeed wear them, called mackinaws and produced from tightly woven wool Melton cloth. Today, several companies make them, and they're all called mackinaws (or sometimes Meltons). But the first mackinaws were sewn by Metis women who lived near the Straits of Mackinac, near present-day Michigan. How did Mackinac become the Mackinaw? That's how the word is pronounced in Canadian French so that's how English speakers wrote it down.

* * *

"Choose to be optimistic; it feels better." —**The Dalai Lama**

It takes 3,000 cows to supply the NFL with enough leather for a year's supply of footba

ALWAYS...

Uncle John's credo: Always follow the advice of experts.

"Always forgive your enemies....
Nothing annoys them so much."
—**Oscar Wilde**

"Always do sober what you said
you'd do drunk. That will teach
you to keep your mouth shut."
—**Ernest Hemingway**

"Always remember before going
on stage, wipe your nose and
check your fly."
—**Alec Guinness**

"Always remember that you
are absolutely unique. Just like
everyone else."
—**Margaret Mead**

"Always hold your head up, but
be careful to keep your nose at a
friendly level."
—**Max L. Forman**

"Always read stuff that will make
you look good if you die in the
middle of it."
—**P. J. O'Rourke**

"Always take hold of things by
the smooth handle."
—**Thomas Jefferson**

"Always dream and shoot higher
than you know you can do. Don't
bother just to be better than your
contemporaries or predecessors.
Try to be better than yourself."
—**William Faulkner**

"Always give a word or a sign of
salute when meeting or passing a
friend, even a stranger."
—**Tecumseh, Shawnee**

"Always listen to experts. They'll
tell you what can't be done and
why. Then do it."
—**Robert Heinlein**

"Always be nice to people on the
way up; because you'll meet the
same people on the way down."
—**Wilson Mizner**

"Always do what you are afraid
to do."
—**Ralph Waldo Emerson**

"Always do right. This will
gratify some people and astonish
the rest."
—**Mark Twain**

The tradition of a man proposing with a gold ring dates as far back as 860 A.D.

NEVER...

Uncle John's credo: Never *follow the advice of experts.*

"Never hire a cleaning lady named Dusty."
—**David Corrado**

"Never trust the advice of a man in difficulties."
—**Aesop**

"Never assume the obvious is true."
—**William Safire**

"Never play peekaboo with a child on a long plane trip. There's no end to the game. Finally, I grabbed him by the bib and said, 'Look, it's always gonna be me!'"
—**Rita Rudner**

"Never pet a porcupine."
—**Kid on *Sesame Street***

"Never send a man to do a horse's job."
—**Mr. Ed**

"Never trust a wolf's tameness, a horse's health, or an enemy's smile."
—**Israel Boone, *Daniel Boone***

"Never trouble trouble till trouble troubles you."
—**John Adams**

"Never give in, never give in, never, never, never, never—in nothing, great or small, large or petty—never give in except to convictions of honor and good sense."
—**Winston Churchill**

"Never spend your money before you have it."
—**Thomas Jefferson**

"Never miss a good chance to shut up."
—**Will Rogers**

"Never get married in the morning, 'cause you may never know who you'll meet that night."
—**Paul Hornung**

"Never explain—your friends do not need it and your enemies will not believe you anyway."
—**Elbert Hubbard**

"Never believe in mirrors or newspapers."
—**Tom Stoppard**

"Never eat more than you can lift."
—**Miss Piggy**

Hair is 88% proteins.

ROLL MODELS

*People who found their 15 minutes of fame thanks to
good deeds performed with…toilet paper.*

ROLL MODEL: THE DEANES
Not long after Matthew and Eliza Deane and their three kids moved to Oakley, Utah, from New Hampshire in August 2014, some teenagers TP'd their new house and front yard with toilet paper. It wasn't the kind of welcome they hoped for, but it wasn't entirely unexpected: "We both lived here as kids and we both did it," Matthew Deane told the *Deseret News*. "It's part of the culture."

What *wasn't* part of the culture—at least when the Deanes were younger—was for the pranksters to do it over and over again. Every Friday and Saturday night for weeks after the Deane family moved in, a dozen or more kids at a time pelted the house with toilet paper. The mess they made was only the beginning: the troublemakers also took apart the Deanes' lawn furniture, rang the doorbell, and pounded on the doors and windows at all hours of the night. Sometimes they drove past the house without stopping, honking their horns and screaming as they went by.

Paper Chase
The Deanes' 15-year-old daughter was so upset by the harassment that she dropped out of high school and had to be homeschooled. Matthew Deane lost more than a few nights of sleep lying in wait for the pranksters to show up so that he could chase after them in his car. Once he cornered a carload of teenagers in a cul-de-sac and told them how upsetting their behavior was to his family. He thought the kids got the message, but the next Friday his house was TP'd again.

Finally, after four months of torment, a sheriff's deputy caught some of the teenagers in the act and took them into custody. Deane could have pressed charges, and perhaps even sued the parents for damages. But he didn't: "It sort of came to me that I should ask these people to bring toilet paper to our house and bring it *into* the house and come to know us," he says.

Roll on Over
Deane figured that if the troublemakers knew his family as people, they'd be less likely to TP the house again. (He was right.) And he thought all that toilet paper could be put to much better use if it was donated to a local charity that works with the poor—that's why he told the kids and their parents to bring some with them.

The first recorded ruler of Japan was a woman…the Empress Himiko (3rd century A.D.).

Even if Deane had only collected toilet paper from those teenagers and their parents, he would have amassed a considerable haul. But when friends and neighbors found out what they were doing, many of them wanted to contribute some toilet paper as well. It wasn't long before the story found its way to the Internet, thanks to Facebook, Twitter, and Matthew Deane's own blog, and soon strangers began sending them packages of toilet paper from all over the country.

On a Roll

The Deanes set an initial goal of collecting 500 rolls of toilet paper by the end of December, then doubled it to 1,000 when their pile grew past 600 rolls. At first they piled the packages of toilet paper in front of the Christmas tree, but so much came in that they had to move it all behind the couch. By New Year's Day 2015 they'd collected more than 1,000 rolls in all, with more arriving daily.

The Deanes had planned to stop collecting toilet paper on New Year's Day, but stopping the donations will probably be as tricky as stopping the TP'ers in the first place. All in all, it's not a bad problem to have. "We just wanted to prove that good will win over all," Deane told the *Deseret News*. "It has become a happy, positive experience. I never thought it would…but it really has."

ROLL MODEL: LEO HILL

Hill, a retired maintenance worker in Denver, Colorado, started on his mission back in 2006 when his wife noticed that rolls of toilet paper sold in packs of four lasted four days, but the same rolls sold in packs of twelve-packs were used up in only three. So Hill started counting the individual sheets of toilet paper he used at every "pit stop," and tallied the figures on flattened toilet paper tubes. After using nine rolls, he found that on average each roll contained 156.75 squares even though the packaging claimed the rolls contained 198 squares—a shortage of 41.25 rolls, or just over 20 percent.

Hill shared his findings with Georgia-Pacific, the company that makes his brand of toilet paper. They thanked him and sent him a coupon for a dozen rolls of toilet paper. When those rolls came up short too, he reported the company to the Denver Business Bureau. No word on whether Hill deserves the credit, but by the time the *Denver Post* repeated his experiment a few years later, all the roll they tested had as many sheets of toilet paper as advertised, and some had up to 10 percent extra. "I'm sure glad you got a good roll," he told the newspaper. "It's really only important when you run out."

NAME YOUR POISON

What's the difference between Scotch and bourbon?
Vodka and gin? Port and sherry? We've always
wondered, so we looked them up.

W HERE ALCOHOL COMES FROM
Ethyl alcohol (the kind you can drink) is created by a process
known as *fermentation.* Yeast is added to fruit juice or a "mash"
(a cooked mixture of grain and water), and the yeast consumes the sugars,
creating two by-products: carbon dioxide and alcohol. But there's a natural limit to this process. When the alcohol content of the mixture reaches
about 15 percent, the yeast loses its ability to convert any more sugars
into alcohol. If you want alcohol with a stronger kick than that, you have
to continue on to a second process: *distillation.*

Distilled spirits are made in a device called a *still,* which consists of a
boiler, a condenser, and a collector. The fermented liquid is heated in the
boiler to at least 173°F, the boiling point for alcohol. All the alcohol (and
some of the water) boils off in the form of vapor. The vapor flows into the
condenser, where it cools back to liquid form and is collected in the collector. The process can be repeated to increase the alcohol content even
further.

All distilled liquor is colorless when it is first made, but it can dark-
en during the aging process, especially when aged in wooden barrels or
casks. Some manufacturers use caramel or artificial coloring to darken
their spirits.

BAR CODES

• **Whiskey.** The word comes from the Gaelic *uisce beatha,* meaning
"water of life." It's alcohol distilled from fermented grains such as barley,
rye, corn, wheat, or a combination. In Ireland and the United States,
whiskey is spelled with an "e." In Scotland, Canada, and Japan, it's
spelled *whisky.*

• **Scotch.** Whiskey made in Scotland. According to international law,
only whiskey made in Scotland may be called Scotch.

• **Bourbon.** American whiskey of the type originally made in Bourbon

County, Kentucky, typically made from 70 percent corn and 30 percent wheat, rye, or other grains. Tennessee whiskey is similar to bourbon, except that it's produced in—you guessed it—Tennessee. It's filtered through a ten-foot layer of maple charcoal, which gives it a milder, distinctive flavor.

• **Brandy.** Alcohol distilled from fermented fruit juices. Brandy is short for brandywine, which comes from the Dutch *brandewijn*, which means "burnt wine." It can be made from grapes, blackberries, apples, plums, or other fruits. Cognac is a type of brandy produced in the Cognac region of France.

• **Gin.** Distilled grain alcohol flavored with juniper berries. Sloe gin is gin flavored with sloe berries from the blackthorn bush instead of juniper berries.

• **Rum.** Alcohol distilled from molasses and sugarcane juice, both of which are by-products of the process used to turn sugarcane into refined sugar.

• **Vodka.** Distilled alcohol originally made from potatoes, but today mostly made from grain. "Vodka" is the diminutive form of *voda*, the Russian word for water, and means "little water." All vodka produced in the United States is required by law to be colorless, odorless, and nearly tasteless, which accounts for its popularity in mixed drinks.

• **Sherry.** White wine that has been fortified by the addition of distilled spirits. It gets its name from *Shareesh*, the Arabic name for the town of Jerez in southwestern Spain, where it originated.

• **Port.** Fortified red or white wine. It gets its name from the city of Porto in northern Portugal, where it originated.

• **Vermouth.** Fortified white wine flavored with aromatic herbs and spices. It's no longer true, but the flavorings were originally used to mask the flavor of inferior wines. Vermouth gets its name from *wermut*, German for wormwood, one of the traditional flavors.

• **Cordials.** Distilled spirits combined with sweetened fruit pulp or fruit juices. Liqueurs are similar to cordials, except that the flavoring is provided by flowers, herbs, seeds, roots, or the bark of plants. Many traditional cordial and liqueur recipes are centuries old and started out as medicinal products.

The word "arena" is from the Latin word for "sand."

LET'S DANCE!

Even non-dancers will like the story behind this dance craze.

THE POLKA

This fast-paced dance is simple to learn, even for Uncle John. And it has a fun origin story, too…depending on who's telling it. The Bohemian version—the one most often cited—claims that in 1834 a young peasant girl named Anna Slezak was bored one Sunday and decided to make up a new dance. She choreographed a hop-step-close-step pattern while singing a Czech folk song ("Uncle Nimra Brought a White Horse"). A local schoolmaster walked by and asked Anna to show it to him; he wrote down the steps and then introduced the polka (from the Czech word *pulka*, meaning "half-step") in ballrooms in nearby Prague. The Polish version is similar: In the 1830s, a Bohemian man was visiting Poland when he saw a little girl dancing the polka (which may actually date as far back as the 1600s) and took the dance back home to Prague, where it was christened *polka*, meaning "Polish woman."

Either way, thanks to the Bohemian army, the dance spread from dance hall to dance hall all over Europe, making it a huge fad in the mid-19th century. Much like rock 'n' roll would be 100 years later, the polka was embraced by the youth culture and vilified by grown-ups, who had only recently accepted the much slower waltz as their dance of choice.

SQUEEZE BOX

For most of the 19th century, polkas were usually written for violins. But as Polish immigrants moved to America in the 20th century, they brought along their accordions (invented around the same time the polka became popular), a much more versatile instrument that allowed a single musician to play melody, harmony, rhythm, and bass—perfect for polka parties. The polka's second golden age took full swing in the Midwest after World War II, where millions of European refugees settled and brought their culture with them. Polka legends such as Frank Yankovic and Lawrence Welk helped legitimize the lively music for adults—many of whom were appalled by rock 'n' roll.

READING TOMBSTONES

In centuries past, families had special symbols carved into gravestones to tell something about their loved ones, to express their grief, or to reflect their faith or belief in eternal life. So, next time you're strolling through a cemetery, look around—the dead are talking to you.

Anchor: Steadfast hope

Tree trunk: The brevity of life

Birds: The soul

Snake in a circle: Everlasting life in heaven (also called *ouroboros*)

Cherub: Divine wisdom or justice

Broken column: An early death

Cross, anchor, and Bible: Faith, hope, and charity

Cross, crown, and palm: Trials, victory, and reward

Crown: Reward and glory

Horseshoe: Protection against evil

Gourds: Deliverance from grief

Lamb: Innocence (usually on a child's grave)

Swallow: Motherhood

Hourglass: Time and its swift flight

Arch: Rejoined with partner in heaven

Ivy: Faithfulness, memory, and undying friendship

Laurel: Victory

Lily: Purity and resurrection

Mermaid: Dualism of Christ—half God, half man

Conch shell: Wisdom

Oak: Strength

Palms: Martyrdom

Shattered urn: Old age

Peacock: Eternal life

Poppy: Eternal sleep

Column: Noble life

Garland: Victory over death

Rooster: Awakening, courage, vigilance

Shell: Birth and resurrection

Six-pointed star: The creator

Olive branch: Forgiveness

Heart: Devotion

Dolphin: Salvation, bearer of souls across water to heaven

Skeleton: Life's brevity

Broken sword: Life cut short

Crossed swords: Life lost in battle

THE BEST DEAL IN $PORT$ HISTORY

When you hear about how much money sports generates for players, owners, and agents, it can make you feel sick—even fed up with the whole sports establishment. But, for some reason, these guys make us smile.

THE A-B-AWAY

In 1974 textile tycoons Ozzie and Dan Silna paid about $1 million for the struggling Carolina Cougars of the American Basketball Association and moved the team to Missouri, where they renamed it the Spirits of St. Louis. Why did they buy the team? Oddly enough, because they knew the league would be going out of business soon. The ABA, just seven years old at the time, was in terrible shape: They couldn't compete with the growing and much more popular National Basketball Association, and ABA teams were losing money or folding altogether. The Silna brothers felt that a merger between the two leagues was probably in the cards, and that some of the more successful ABA teams would become NBA teams, a potentially lucrative opportunity. So they beefed up the Spirits with great young players—Moses Malone and Don Chaney among them—and waited for the league to collapse. In 1976 it did, and the NBA moved in. One problem: They didn't want the Spirits.

THE DEAL

The ABA was down to just six teams by this point (the NBA had 18), but the bigger league wanted only four of them—the Denver Rockets (later the Nuggets), the Indiana Pacers, the New York (later New Jersey) Nets, and the San Antonio Spurs. The two they didn't want: the Kentucky Colonels and the Spirits. Luckily, that didn't leave the Silnas and the Colonels' owner John Y. Brown powerless: For the merger to go through, every owner had to agree with whatever deal was hammered out. The NBA dealt with the Colonels by offering Brown a $3.3 million "buyout"—and he took it. They offered the same to the Silnas...but they declined. They had other ideas.

On top of the $3.3 million, the Silnas, along with their bulldog of an attorney, Donald Schupak, demanded one-seventh of future television revenues generated by the four former ABA teams. At the time, television revenues for pro basketball games were relatively miniscule—the league had terrible ratings compared to pro baseball and football. So the NBA, after negotiating the lump-sum payment down to $2.2 million, agreed. It was a mistake that they regret to this day.

SPIRITS IN THE MATERIAL WORLD

For the first few years, the Silnas made less than $100,000 per year from the TV deal. That's not bad for doing nothing, but it was about to get a lot better. The legendary rivalry between Larry Bird's Boston Celtics and Magic Johnson's Los Angeles Lakers, starting in 1980, fueled a huge growth in the NBA's popularity—and in TV revenues. By 1982 the Silnas were making almost $200,000 a year. The league offered the brothers $5 million to buy out their contract. They said they'd take $8 million, but the NBA refused—which was probably a dumber move than when it made the original deal. In 1984 Michael Jordan entered the league; by 1988 the Silnas were getting nearly $1 million per year. In 1992 the league offered them $18 million to end the contract. No way. By 1994 their earnings were up to around $4 million annually. And it gets still better.

SLAM DUNK

Business experts have called the Silna brothers' 1976 contract possibly the best in history—and not just in sports, but in all business. And the most significant clause in it: "The right to receive such revenues shall continue for as long as the NBA or its successors continue in its existence."

As of 2014, the former owners of the former team known as the Spirits of St. Louis had raked in an estimated $300 million in total. The NBA negotiated a settlement of $500 million *more* that year, with a much smaller ongoing revenue stream for the brothers. That brought their total up to more than $800 million...for an initial investment of about $5 million. "I would have loved to have an NBA team," says 73-year-old Ozzie Silna. "But if I look at it retrospectively over what I would have gotten, versus what I've received now—then I'm a happy camper."

First people to use sails on their ships: the ancient Phoenicians (around 2000 B.C.).

SOUND SMARTER

Experts say the path to success is built on a good vocabulary. Here are a few words, with examples of their use, that might make you sound smart enough to go into politics. (Hmm...maybe that was a bad example.)

New Word: Endemic (en-DEM-ik)
Meaning: Belonging to a particular region or people
Instead of... "Them Tasmanian Devils are only found in Tazakistan, I'm pretty sure. And zoos."
Sound Smarter: "The Tasmanian Devil is *endemic* only to the Australian island of Tasmania."

New Word: Cavil (KAV-uhl)
Meaning: To quibble or nitpick
Instead of... "Well, I guess that's for the jury to decide."
Sound Smarter: "I hate to *cavil*, darling, but I'm fairly sure that man you just hit was riding a Segway, not a scooter."

New Word: Parlous (PAHR-lous)
Meaning: Dangerous
Instead of... "This won't hurt a bit!"
Sound Smarter: "I assure you there is nothing *parlous* about the intracranial demulsification procedure."

New Word: Imbibe (im-BAHYB)
Meaning: Drink; absorb
Instead of... "Let's go sit on the porch, down a few cold ones and take in the scenery."
Sound Smarter: "Please join me on the veranda to *imbibe* some refreshing beverages and enjoy the spectacular ocean view."

New Word: Soporific (soh-puh-RIF-ik)
Meaning: Sleep-inducing
Instead of... "I could eat a whole 'nuther helping of pie—but I'm just too pooped."
Sound Smarter: "Unfortunately, the *soporific* effects of the turkey, not to

first Allied bomb dropped on Berlin in WWII killed the only elephant in the Berlin Zoo.

mention all the wine I've imbibed, prevent me from staying awake long enough to partake of dessert."

New Word: Alacrity (uh-LAK-ri-tee)
Meaning: Quick, cheerful enthusiasm
Instead of... "Brian's a go-getter, isn't he? I like him. But he kind of bugs me, too."
Sound Smarter: "Brian's tendency to approach every task with *alacrity* made him not only one of the office's favorite employees, but also one of the most annoying."

New Word: Circumspect (SUR-kuhm-spekt)
Meaning: Cautious
Instead of... "Uh, Fred, you might not want to look down that tube."
Sound Smarter: "Frederick, a more *circumspect* approach to that fireworks cannon you just lit might be advisable."

New Word: Phlegmatic (fleg-MAT-ik)
Meaning: Apathetic; sluggish
Instead of... "Get your lazy butt up off the sofa and answer the phone yourself."
Sound Smarter: "*Guinness World Records* just called to let you know you've been named Most *Phlegmatic* Couch Potato."

New Word: Enmity (EN-mi-tee)
Meaning: Ill will, hostility, or outright hatred
Instead of... "I hate you! I hate, hate, hate you!"
Sound Smarter: "Be assured, my charming friend, that my *enmity* for you is outmatched only by my resistance to having my tonsils extracted through my nasal passages."

New Word: Temerity (teh-MEHR-eh-tee)
Meaning: Foolhardiness; reckless courage
Instead of... "I don't know if that was brave or just stupid, what you just did. Did it really eat your cell phone?"
Sound Smarter: "It takes extreme *temerity* to jump into the grizzly bear enclosure, Jethro. Shall I call an ambulance?"

Studies show: The aroma of fresh-baked goods makes customers spend more money.

I CURSE YOU!

*Save these classic curses to use against
people who refuse to toast you.*

May the curse of Mary Maline and her nine blind children chase you so far over the hills of Damnation that the Lord himself won't find you with a telescope.

May your daughter's beauty be admired by everyone in the circus.

May the devil cut the head off you and make a day's work of your neck.

Six horse-loads of graveyard clay upon you.

May I live just long enough to bury you.

May you be afflicted with the itch and have no nails to scratch with.

All your teeth should fall out except one, and you should have a toothache in that one.

May the seven terriers of hell sit on the spool of your breast and bark in at your soul-case.

May you be transformed into a chandelier, to hang by day and burn by night.

May you win a lottery and spend it all on doctors.

May the devil swallow you sideways.

May you live in a house of 100 rooms, and may each room have its own bed, and may you wander every night from room to room, and from bed to bed, unable to sleep.

May you go stone-blind so that you can't tell your wife from a haystack.

Your nose should grow so much hair it strains your soup.

May fire and brimstone never fail to fall in showers on you.

May you have devoted children to chase the flies off your nose.

May you back into a pitchfork and grab a hot stove for support.

May those who love us love us. And those that don't love us, may God turn their hearts, and if He cannot turn their hearts, may He turn their ankles so we'll know them by their limping.

The guillotine was used as a method of execution in France until 1977.

THE ENGLISH LANGUAGE

*If English is your first language, thank your lucky stars
that you didn't have to learn it as a second language.*

"Any language where the unassuming word 'fly' signifies an annoying insect, a means of travel, and a critical part of a gentleman's apparel is clearly asking to be mangled."
—**Bill Bryson**

"It's a strange language in which skating on thin ice can get you into hot water."
—**Franklin P. Jones**

"English has created the word 'loneliness' to express the pain of being alone. And it has created the word 'solitude' to express the glory of being alone."
—**Paul Tillich**

"Not only does the English language borrow words from other languages, it sometimes chases them down dark alleys, hits them over the head, and goes through their pockets."
—**Eddy Peters**

"Introducing 'Lite'—the new way to spell 'Light', but with twenty percent fewer letters."
—**Jerry Seinfeld**

"When I read some of the rules for writing the English language correctly, I think any fool can make a rule, and every fool will mind it."
—**Henry David Thoreau**

"If the English language made any sense, 'lackadaisical' would have something to do with a shortage of flowers."
—**Doug Larson**

"The English language is like a broad river on whose bank a few patient anglers are sitting, while, higher up, the stream is being polluted by a string of refuse-barges tipping out their muck."
—**Cyril Connolly**

"Even if you do learn to speak correct English, whom are you going to speak it to?"
—**Clarence Darrow**

"Do not compute the totality of your poultry population until all the manifestations of incubation have been entirely completed."
—**William Jennings Bryan**

According to scientists, octopuses do not have eight legs. They have six arms and two l

PERSONAL SPACE

There's not much room on space vehicles, but NASA allows astronauts up to 1.5 pounds of personal items. Here's what went up on these flights.

• To note the historical significance of the first flight to the Moon, the *Apollo 11* crew brought a piece of wood from the Wright brothers' 1903 airplane.

• In 2008 the space shuttle *Atlantis* carried three NASCAR starter flags, commemorating the 50th anniversary of the Daytona 500. One of the flags was given to that year's Daytona winner, Ryan Newman.

• The 1971 *Apollo 15* voyage took University of Michigan alumni-chapter documents to the Moon—so now the school can claim it has a branch on the Moon.

• Cornell University founder Ezra Cornell wore a pair of tan silk socks on his wedding day in 1831. In 1990 Cornell graduate G. David Low boarded the space shuttle… carrying Cornell's socks.

• The space shuttle *Atlantis* (March 2007) brought a lead cargo tag from Jamestown colony in honor of the history of American exploration.

• In 2011 flight engineer Satoshi Furukawa represented Japan on the International Space Station. His item: a box of LEGO bricks. He used them to make a replica of the ISS.

• In 2008 Garrett Reisman, a New York Yankees fan, brought a vial of dirt from Yankee Stadium onto *Discovery*.

• Pete Conrad took matching beanie hats for his crew on *Apollo 12* in 1969. Well, not entirely matching, because Conrad's had a propeller.

• Gregory Johnson (*Endeavour*, 2008) took the title page of *Expedition 6*, actor Bill Pullman's play about life on the International Space Station.

• Pilot John Young was reprimanded for sneaking a corned beef sandwich onto the 1965 *Gemini 3* flight. Crumbs are hazardous on a space capsule. (Space food is crumb-free.)

• The 2007 space shuttle *Discovery* carried the prop lightsaber used by Mark Hamill (Luke Skywalker) in *Star Wars*—a fake space relic in real space.

THE *OTHER* SOPRANOS

*If you're a man, perhaps you need a little reminder
that your life is pretty good. Well, just be glad you
weren't born in Italy in the 1700s. (Now cross
your legs and read this story.)*

THE ULTIMATE SACRIFICE

Who were the *castrati*? They were boys who were castrated in an effort to fill the Catholic Church's need for singing talent. The practice appeared in Europe as early as the 1500s, but historians estimate that between 1720 and 1730 (the height of the craze), 4,000 boys between the ages of nine and twelve who showed even vague musical promise were castrated each year. By that time, the practice was limited almost entirely to Italy, but its seeds had been planted years earlier when the Church, having banned women from singing in choirs (religious officials thought women's voices were too seductive for the church) turned to young boys, whose sweet tones were preferable to the shrill soprano falsettists.

Castration prevented puberty, and without the male hormone *testosterone*, a castrato's vocal cords remained small and immature throughout his lifetime, which kept his voice high. And because his bone joints didn't harden, he also grew unusually tall and developed a large chest cavity, which gave him extra lung capacity. With rigorous training, the combined effect was tremendous vocal flexibility, a high range, pure tone, and extraordinary endurance. The very best could hold a note for up to a minute without taking a breath.

THE GOOD LIFE

Many poor parents willingly sacrificed their sons to this cause in the hope that they'd find fame and fortune. Cardinals, church fathers, choir directors, and composers signed up the castrati for shows and performances. The boys dedicated their youth to a rigorous musical and vocal training regime. But only a few went on to stardom. The rest made careers in cathedrals, church choirs, and the theater.

Many historians consider the castrati who did make it "the original pop stars." Women swooned for them onstage and off; one young castrato

---

Britons began milking cows at least 6,000 years ago.

was welcomed to the city of Florence by the town's wealthiest and most influential citizens. And though their voices were as high as a soprano's, they rarely played women's roles in operas—they were cast instead as the brave young heroes. (Male sopranos played the female roles until women were allowed on the stage in the late 18th century.)

BEST OF THE BEST

At their peak the castrati were employed by all of Europe's opera houses and church choirs, and the century's biggest composers, such as George Frideric Handel and Christoph Willibald von Gluck, wrote operas and vocal music specifically with castrato voices in mind. And the singers demanded enormous annual salaries: Records show some being paid as much as £1,500 (the equivalent of about $245,000 today).

The most famous castrati of them all: Carlo Maria Broschi (1705–82)—known on the stage as Farinelli. He was hired by the king of Spain, Ferdinand VI, for an undisclosed (but assumed to be very large) sum of money to serenade the king every night beneath his bedroom window. Ferdinand credited the youthful-sounding singer with single-handedly lifting his depressed spirits and helping him find the mental strength to attend to his affairs of state. Farinelli worked for the royal family for the next 25 years.

DOWNFALL OF THE DRAMA QUEENS

The reign of the castrati waned in Italy by the mid-1800s. The Catholic Church had long condemned the practice (and threatened to excommunicate participants), and, bowing to public opinion, the Italian government made castration illegal in 1870.

But historians say that it was largely the conceit of the castrati themselves that brought about their demise. Most of the performers became spoiled and egotistical; they often changed the scores to highlight their voices. Leading composers Rossini, Wagner, and Verdi all grew frustrated with their tampering and simply stopped writing for them. At the same time, the devoted but temperamental opera-loving public lost interest in the castrati, turning instead to the female soprano, whose timbre had become fashionable. Alessandro Moreschi, the world's last professional castrato and director of papal music for the Vatican, died in 1922. (Recordings of him are still widely available.)

About 1 in 4 American employees say they're always angry on the job.

WEIRD MEXICO

*The odd, the weird, the strange, and
the crazy—south of the border.*

WORMING AROUND

One of the most lucrative products (and exports) in Mexico is mescal, a liquor similar to tequila, and most commonly packaged with a worm in every bottle. Legend says that eating the worm triggers powerful hallucinations. In 2005 the Mexican government considered banning worms from mescal. Because of the hallucinations? Nope. The worm is too high in fat, they claim. (The proposal failed; the worm remains.)

El LOCO

In 1993 Gerardo Palomero went on an animal-rights crusade, invading Mexico City slaughterhouses and yelling at meat cutters to treat animals more humanely. While workers respected his message, they found Palomero hard to take seriously because he was dressed in the brightly colored spandex costume of his professional wrestling character, "Super Animal."

THE OLDEST PROFESSION

In 2005 women's groups in Mexico City raised funds to build a home for elderly prostitutes. The city government even donated a building. But it's not a retirement home—it's a brothel. Hopeful "resident" Gloria Maria, 74, said, "I can't charge what the young ones do, but I still have two or three clients a day."

SHE KNOWS WHAT SHE'S TALKING ABOUT

In December 1998, newly elected Mexico City mayor Rosario Robles Berlanga was preparing to give an inauguration speech in which she planned to announce a crackdown on crime. Just hours before Berlanga was to speak, her top aide was mugged in a taxi. The thief stole the briefcase containing the mayor's tough-on-crime speech.

CHOOSE YOUR WORDS CAREFULLY

*Uncle John can never remember without looking it up that Washington, DC,
is the capit<u>al</u>, and the building where Congress meets is the Capit<u>ol</u>.
Here are some more word pairs that drive him crazy.*

FLAUNT...or...FLOUT?

• *To flaunt* something is to display it ostentatiously. When people flaunt their wealth, they are showing off to impress others or make them envious.

• To *flout* something, such as a rule or a law, means to openly disregard it, often in a mocking or contemptuous fashion.

PRESCRIBE...OR...PROSCRIBE?

• *Prescribe* means to authorize or establish something as a rule or a guide, such as when a doctor prescribes medication to a patient.

• *Proscribe* means to forbid or denounce. Example: Smoking is proscribed in most government buildings; if you want to smoke, you have to step outside.

ENORMITY...OR...ENORMOUSNESS?

• *Enormity* refers to the large scale of something evil or morally wrong, such as the enormity of a murderer's crimes.

• When describing the giant size of something in a context where no negative moral judgment is implied, believe it or not, the correct word to use is *enormousness* (or, if that sounds too weird, *immensity*). Though it's common for people to use the word *enormity* in a neutral context—"the *enormity* of the task at hand," for example—purists consider this usage to be incorrect.

COMPLIMENT...OR...COMPLEMENT?

• *Compliment* means to express praise or admiration.

• *Complement* means to add to something in a way that improves it, such as when an attractive scarf or necktie *complements* an outfit.

A whale of a trip: On a week-long cruise, the average traveler gains 8 pounds.

ADVERSE...OR...AVERSE

• *Adverse* means "harmful, unfavorable, or inhibiting success," and is applied to situations or conditions. Prolonged drought, for example, has an *adverse* effect on crop yields.

• *Averse* means "opposing or having a strong dislike," and usually describes someone's attitude. A person's shyness makes them *averse* to reading their own writing aloud. (Note: Because the Latin origin of *averse* means "turn from," purists prefer "averse from," but "averse to" is more commonly used.)

ENSURE...OR...INSURE?

• *Ensure* and *insure* are largely interchangeable. Both mean "to make certain that something will happen." Putting on a coat can both ensure *and* insure that you will be warm when you go outside.

• The words are not interchangeable where insurance policies are concerned: people can buy *insurance*, but they can't buy *ensurance*.

PRECIPITATE...OR...PRECIPITOUS

• *Precipitate* can mean to cause something to happen suddenly or prematurely— the spilled drink precipitated a barroom brawl. It can also refer to rain.

• *Precipitous*, on the other hand, means steep. Example: In 2008 there was a precipitous drop in U.S. home sales.

DISCREET...OR...DISCRETE

• When someone is *discreet*, they are being cautious and showing good judgment

• When something is *discrete*, it is separate and distinct from other things. The individual pieces of a jigsaw puzzle, for example, are discrete objects that are placed together to complete the puzzle.

COUNCIL...OR...COUNSEL

• A *council* is a group of people who serve as administrators or advisors.

• To *counsel* someone means to give them advice or to recommend a course of action. In the legal profession, attorneys on opposing sides of a court case are called *counsels* for the prosecution and for the defense. The advice given can als be referred to as counsel.

CELEBRITY LAWSUITS

*Uncle John noticed that a number of the cases in our
"Strange Lawsuits" file involve celebrities of one
sort or another. Here's a sampling.*

THE PLAINTIFF: Mark Twain

THE DEFENDANT: Estes and Lauriat Publishing Co.

THE LAWSUIT: In 1876 the Canadian publishers pirated the text of Twain's book *Tom Sawyer* and put out a low-priced edition. It cut into legitimate U.S. sales and deprived Twain of royalties. When he wrote *The Adventures of Huckleberry Finn* in 1884, he was determined to prevent a recurrence. He decided to publish *Huck Finn* himself...but hold off printing it until he had orders for 40,000 copies. That way, the book pirates wouldn't have a chance to undercut him.

Yet somehow, Estes and Lauriat got hold of a manuscript and started selling a pirated edition two months *before* Twain's authorized edition was available. Livid, Twain sued them.

THE VERDICT: Believe it or not, Twain lost the case. He issued this statement: "[The judge has allowed the publisher] to sell property which does not belong to him but me—property which he has not bought and I have not sold. Under this same ruling, I am now advertising the judge's homestead for sale; and if I make as good a sum out of it as I expect, I shall go on and sell the rest of his property."

THE PLAINTIFFS: Ten people named Jeff Stone, including the mayor of Temecula, California; a guy who works for NASA; and Paul Peterson—who isn't actually a Jeff Stone, but played a character with that name on TV's *Donna Reed Show* from 1958 to 1966

THE DEFENDANT: Jeff Gillooly, Tonya Harding's infamous ex-husband, who served seven months in jail for plotting the 1994 attack on her skating rival, Nancy Kerrigan

THE LAWSUIT: In 1995 Gillooly filed to change his name to Jeff Stone (so he could have some anonymity). Other Jeff Stones announced that they were outraged. Mayor Stone said his "hard-earned good name would be sullied"; Peterson insisted Gillooly was mocking his sitcom;

Fewer than 50 pilgrims survived their first winter in America.

NASA's Stone spread the word that he simply didn't want to share his name with Gillooly. And then they sued to prevent it.

THE VERDICT: In a 10-minute hearing, the judge ruled there was no basis for stopping Gillooly from becoming a Jeff Stone.

THE PLAINTIFF: Saddam Hussein
THE DEFENDANT: *Le Nouvel Observateur*, a French magazine
THE LAWSUIT: In an article about Hussein, the magazine described him as a "monster," "executioner," "complete cretin," and a "noodle." Hussein sued for libel.
THE VERDICT: Case dismissed.

THE PLAINTIFF: A dentist
THE DEFENDANTS: Johnny Carson and NBC
THE LAWSUIT: In the early 1980s, during a broadcast of the *Tonight Show*, Carson mentioned he'd seen a report saying that dentists were closing their offices due to lack of business. "News like this," he quipped, "hasn't made me so happy since I heard the Gestapo disbanded." An angry dentist immediately sued Carson and the station for $1 million for libel.
THE VERDICT: Case dismissed.

THE PLAINTIFF: Dustin Hoffman
THE DEFENDANT: *Los Angeles* magazine
THE LAWSUIT: In its March 1997 issue, the magazine superimposed a picture of Hoffman's face—from the film *Tootsie*, in which he dressed as a woman—on a the body of a model "wearing a smashing gown and smart high heels." The caption: "Dustin Hoffman isn't a drag in a butter-colored silk gown by Richard Tyler and Ralph Lauren heels." Hoffman sued for $5 million, saying they had turned him into "an unpaid fashion model."
THE VERDICT: Calling Hoffman "one of our greatest living treasures," the judge ordered the magazine to pay the actor $3 million.

Scientific term for foul-smelling breath (worse than "bad" breath): *ozostomia*.

REJECTED!

If you gave up every time you failed, you'd never succeed. These people got rejected, but they didn't give up—and the rest of us benefited.

W ho wants to copy a document on plain paper?"
This was included in one of the 20 rejection letters Chester
Carlson received for his invention—the Xerox machine. After
six years of rejections, the Haloid Company bought his idea in 1944.
The first copier was sold in 1950, and Carlson made over $150 million in
his lifetime.

"The product is worthless."
Bayer Pharmaceuticals' 1897 rejection of Felix Hoffman's formula for
aspirin. (They eventually accepted it in 1899.)

**"Too different from other juvenile titles on the market to warrant its
selling."**
One book publisher said this in 1937 about *And to Think That I Saw It on
Mulberry Street*, the first children's book by Dr. Seuss. In fact, 27 publishers rejected it before Vanguard Press accepted. Dr. Seuss went on to write
over 40 children's books that sold nearly half a billion copies.

"Balding, skinny, can dance a little."
Paramount Pictures made this assessment after an early audition by Fred
Astaire. He signed with RKO Studios instead.

**"We are not interested in science fiction which deals with negative
utopias. They do not sell."**
This was said to Stephen King in the early 1970s about his first novel,
Carrie. The book went on to become the first of dozens of bestsellers for
King, the top-selling horror author of all time.

"Hopeless."
A music teacher's opinion of his student's composing ability. The student:
Ludwig van Beethoven.

"BUNGA BUNGA!"

Sophomoric clown or a brilliant satirist of British imperialism? Either way,
Horace de Vere Cole was responsible for one of the best pranks in history.

HIS MAJESTY REQUESTS...

In the years before World War I, Britain had the most powerful navy in the world. And the HMS *Dreadnought*, armed with 10 large guns and powered by a steam engine, was the pride of the fleet. Considered the superweapon of its day, the huge battleship lay anchored under the tightest security in Weymouth. Few outside the Navy's top officers had ever stepped on board, much less toured its "top-secret" state-of-the-art weaponry.

On February 10, 1910, Sir William May, the ship's captain, received a telegram from the Foreign Office, signed by Under-Secretary Sir Charles Hardinge, announcing the impending arrival of the emperor of Abyssinia and his court in England. The emperor was to receive the royal treatment, including a tour of the HMS *Dreadnought*. The captain immediately ordered his officers and crew to prepare to greet the emperor with all due pomp and circumstance. Guns were polished, decks swabbed, and uniforms washed and pressed in anticipation of the royal tour.

V.I.P. TREATMENT

But the telegram was a fake—it was sent by a practical joker named Horace de Vere Cole. A few days later, he and five co-conspirators (including author Virginia Woolf and her brother) blackened their faces and hands with burnt cork, glued false beards to their chins, donned long red robes topped with makeshift turbans (all rented), and took a cab to London's Paddington Station. Brazenly declaring that he was a state official named "Herbert Cholmondley," Cole talked the stationmaster into giving them a VIP train to Weymouth, where the delegation was met with a full honor guard and a brass band.

An Abyssinian flag couldn't be found (no one knew what one looked like), so one from Zanzibar was used instead. And the band played the Zanzibar national anthem, since that was the only African anthem they knew. (The pranksters didn't know the difference.) The Navy had no translator either: fortunately, the delegation supplied their own, and his

---

Two years after Jan and Dean's "Dead Man's Curve" became a hit, Jan Berry nearly die

translations were so eloquent that none of the navy officers noticed that the language spoken by the "Abyssinians" bore a striking resemblance to fractured Latin. And as they were shown all of the ship's accoutrements, they shouted "Bunga Bunga!" in approval at everything they saw.

There were a few anxious moments. One was when the pranksters realized one of the Navy officers knew Woolf. But the officer never caught on. Another came when their "interpreter" sneezed and almost blew off his whiskers. Again, no one noticed. Weather almost sank the prank, too: Rain began to fall as the delegation arrived at the *Dreadnought*; Cole managed to talk their way onto a lower deck just as their makeup started to run.

Finally, Cole decided it was time to get out. They refused lunch (they weren't sure what dietary restrictions might go along with their made-up religion) and left quickly on the excuse that there were no prayer mats for their daily devotionals.

The delegation was given a military escort back to their train. Still in disguise and under Naval supervision, the "Abyssinians" requested that waiters serving them dinner wear white gloves. (The train stopped and was held up in Reading to purchase the gloves.)

SHIP OF FOOLS

Five days later a photograph appeared in the *Daily Mirror*, showing the "Abyssinian" delegation with their Naval hosts. In the accompanying article, Cole exposed the hoax and ridiculed the Navy for being so gullible. All over London, sailors were harassed with cries of "Bunga Bunga!" The Admiralty was furious, but its attempt to charge Cole and his party with treason (the delegation had seen top-secret areas of the ship) was hooted down in Parliament and the press. After all, as people pointed out, the only "treasonous" thing they'd done was make the Admiralty and its officers look like fools. Besides, the only actual crime committed was sending a telegram under a fake name.

The Navy decided to not press charges, but still felt that somebody had to be punished. As the pranksters were all upper class, they could get away with a symbolic act to settle the dispute as gentlemen. Naval officers visited Cole and gave him six symbolic taps on the buttocks with a cane. Cole insisted he be allowed to do the same to the officers. Amazingly, the officers agreed.

...in a car accident three blocks from Dead Man's Curve in Los Angeles.

UNIQUELY PRESIDENTIAL

You may know that Richard Nixon was the only U.S. president to resign or that Grover Cleveland was the only president to serve two non-consecutive terms. But there are many more presidential anomalies than that.

The president: Jimmy Carter
Notable achievement: First president to write a children's book. Carter wrote *The Little Baby Snoogle-Fleejer*, which was illustrated by his daughter Amy, and published in 1995. The plot: A crippled boy named Jeremy meets a repulsive sea monster who turns out to be quite friendly.

The president: Abraham Lincoln
Notable achievement: Only president to earn a patent. In 1849 Lincoln invented a type of buoy. Lincoln is also the only U.S. president to have worked as a bartender.

The president: Theodore Roosevelt
Notable achievement: Only president to be blind in one eye. Roosevelt took a hard punch to his left eye in a boxing match. It detached the retina, leaving Roosevelt blind in his left eye for the rest of his life. The boxing match occurred in 1908, while Roosevelt was president.

The president: Richard Nixon
Notable achievement: Only president to have been a carny. When he was a teenager, Richard Nixon was a midway barker at the Slippery Gulch Rodeo in Arizona.

The president: Gerald Ford
Notable achievement: Only president to survive two assassination attempts in the same month. In September 1975, former Charles Manson follower Lynette "Squeaky" Fromme tried to shoot Ford when he reached out to shake her hand in a public meet-and-greet. She pulled the trigger, but the gun's chamber was empty. Just three weeks later another woman, Sara Jane Moore, fired on Ford in a similar crowd situation, but a bystander knocked her arm away.

Brooke Shields, Teri Garr, and John Travolta all appeared in 1970s Band-Aid commercials

NOVEL STARTS

Were you really just resting your eyes in high school lit class? Below are the first lines of classic works by famous authors. If you need a lifeline, the titles are listed on the next page. (Answers on page 194.)

1. "Early in the spring of 1750, in the village of Juffure, four days upriver from the coast of Gambia, West Africa, a man-child was born to Omoro and Binta Kinte."

2. "He was an old man who fished alone in a skiff in the Gulf stream and he had gone 84 days now without taking a fish."

3. "When Mary Lennoz was sent to Misselthwaite Manor to live with her uncle, everybody said she was the most disagreeable-looking child ever seen."

4. "Who is John Galt?"

5. "It was a pleasure to burn."

6. "You will rejoice to hear that no disaster has accompanied the commencement of an enterprise which you have regarded with such evil forebodings."

7. "TOM!"

8. "It was a bright cold day in April, and the clocks were striking thirteen."

9. "As Gregor Samsa awoke one morning from uneasy dreams, he found himself transformed into a giant insect."

10. "Call me Ishmael."

11. "Whether I turn out to be the hero of my own life, or whether that station will be held by anybody else, these pages must show."

12. "Buck did not read the newspapers or he would have known that trouble was brewing, not alone for himself, but for every tide-water

dog, strong of muscle and with warm, long hair, from Puget Sound to San Diego."

13. "1801—I have just returned from a visit to my landlord—the solitary neighbor that I shall be troubled with."

14. "Well, Prince, so Genoa and Hucca are now just family estates of the Buonapartes..."

15. "Last night I dreamt I went to Manderly again."

16. "In my younger and more vulnerable years, my father gave me some advice that I've been turning over in my mind ever since."

17. "The cold passed reluctantly from the earth, and the retiring fogs revealed an army stretched out on the hills, resting."

18. "3 May. Bistritz. Left Munich at 8:35 P.M., on 1st May, arriving at Vienna early next morning; should have arrived at 6:46, but train was an hour late."

19. "You better not even tell nobody but God."

20. "It is a truth universally acknowledged, that a single man in possession of a good fortune, must be in want of a wife."

The Adventures of Tom Sawyer (Mark Twain)
Atlas Shrugged (Ayn Rand)
The Call of the Wild (Jack London)
The Color Purple (Alice Walker)
David Copperfield (Charles Dickens)
Dracula (Bram Stoker)
Fahrenheit 451 (Ray Bradbury)
Frankenstein (Mary Shelley)
The Great Gatsby (F. Scott Fitzgerald)
Metamorphosis (Franz Kafka)
Moby Dick (Herman Melville)

1984 (George Orwell)
The Old Man and the Sea (Ernest Hemingway)
Pride and Prejudice (Jane Austen)
Rebecca (Daphne du Maurier)
The Red Badge of Courage (Stephen Crane)
Roots (Alex Haley)
The Secret Garden (Francis Hodgson Burnett)
War and Peace (Leo Tolstoy)
Wuthering Heights (Emily Brontë)

Favorite candy of the Netherlands: *drop*. What is it? Salty licorice.

MYTH-SPOKEN

We hate to say it (well actually, we like to say it), but some of the best-known quotes in history weren't said by the people they're attributed to...and some weren't even said at all!

Line: "Go west, young man, go west."
Supposedly Said By: Horace Greeley, publisher of the *New York Tribune*, in 1851
Actually: Even in 1851, big-city media had all the influence. Greeley merely reprinted an article from the Terre Haute, Indiana, *Express*, but ever since, people have identified it with him. The line was really written by a "now forgotten and never very famous" newspaperman named John Soule.

Line: "Taxation without representation is tyranny!"
Supposedly Said By: James Otis, a lawyer arguing in a Boston court against British search warrants, in 1761
Actually: For years, schoolchildren were taught that this was "the rallying cry of the American Revolution." But no one in Otis's time ever mentioned him saying it. It wasn't until 1820, almost 60 years later, that John Adams referred to the phrase for the first time.

Line: "This is a great wall!"
Supposedly Said By: President Richard Nixon
Actually: It's one of the lines used to denigrate Nixon...and he *did* say it to Chinese officials in 1972 when he saw the Great Wall for the first time. But it's a bum rap. As Paul Boller and John George write in *They Never Said It*:

> This was not his complete sentence, and out of context it sounds silly. It is only fair to put it back into its setting: "When one stands here," Nixon declared, "and sees the wall going to the peak of this mountain and realizes it runs for hundreds of miles—as a matter of fact, thousands of miles—over the mountains and through the valleys of this country and that it was built over 2,000 years ago, I think you would have to conclude that this is a great wall and that it had to be built by a great people."

Feeding dyes to hens will change the color of their eggs' yolks.

Line: "Let them eat cake."

Supposedly Said By: Marie Antoinette, Queen of France, when she was told that conditions were so bad that the peasants had no bread to eat

Actually: She was alleged to have said it just before the French Revolution. But the phrase had already been used by then. It has been cited as an old parable by philosopher Henri Rousseau in 1778—a decade or so before Marie Antoinette supposedly said it. Chances are, it was a rumor spread by her political enemies.

Line: "There are three kinds of lies: lies, damn lies, and statistics."

Supposedly Said By: Mark Twain

Actually: Twain, one of America's most quotable writers, was quoting someone else: Prime Minister Benjamin Disraeli of England.

Line: "Keep the government poor and remain free."

Supposedly Said By: Justice Oliver Wendell Holmes

Actually: Ronald Reagan said it during a speech and attributed the line to Holmes. But Holmes never said it, and it wasn't written by a speechwriter, either. Reagan's "speechwriting office" later told a reporter, "He came up with that one himself."

*   *   *

HOLY BAT FACTS!

• Most species of bats live 12 to 15 years, but some live as long as 30 years. Some species can fly as fast as 60 miles per hour and as high as 10,000 feet.

• Bats are social animals and live in colonies in caves. The colonies can get huge: Bracken Cave in Texas contains an estimated 20 million Mexican free-tailed bats.

• Vampire bats drink blood through a "drinking straw" that the bat makes with its tongue and lower lip. The bats' saliva contains an anticoagulant that keeps blood flowing by impeding the formation of blood clots.

• It's not uncommon for a vampire bat to return to the same animal night after night, weakening and eventually killing it.

An Atlanta, Georgia, law forbids "smelly people" from riding on public streetcars.

WHY DON'T WE HAVE A WORD FOR THAT?

*Americans excel at inventing colorful expressions and slang,
but it turns out other countries are pretty good at it, too.*

Kummerspeck (Germany): "Grief bacon"—the weight you gain by overeating when you're worried about something.

Attaccabottoni (Italy): A "buttonholer"—someone who corners casual acquaintances or even complete strangers for the purpose of telling them their miserable life stories.

Modré Pondeli (Czech): "Blue Monday"—When you skip coming in to work to give yourself a three-day weekend.

Razbliuto (Russia): The feeling you have for a person you used to love, but don't anymore.

Shitta (Iran): Leftover dinner that's eaten for breakfast.

Tartle (Scotland): To momentarily forget the name of the person you're talking to. The word helps reduce the social embarrassment of such situations: "I'm sorry, I tartled there for a moment."

Pana po'o (Hawaii): To scratch your head in an attempt to remember something you've forgotten.

Ngaobera (Easter Island): A sore throat caused by too much screaming.

Backpfeifengesicht (Germany): A face that's just begging for somebody to put their fist in it.

Papierkrieg (Germany): "Paper war"—bureaucratic paperwork whose only purpose is to block you from getting the refund, insurance payment, or other benefit that you have coming.

Rujuk (Indonesia): To remarry your ex-wife.

Mokita (New Guinea): The truth that everyone knows, but no one will speak about.

Gorrero (Spain, Central America): Someone who never picks up the check.

Fucha (Poland): Using your employer's time and resources for your own purposes. (Uncle John had never heard of such a thing and wanted to ask around the office if anyone else had, but everyone is still out to lunch.)

How about you? 85% of Americans have Rh positive blood.

HE'S A CURLY WOLF

Real cowboy slang of the late 19th century was a lot different from the way it's been depicted in movies and on TV. Some examples:

Coffee boiler: A lazy person who sits around the coffee pot instead of helping with the work.

Big bug: Important person; big shot.

Bone orchard: Cemetery.

The boss: The best.

He only gave it a lick and a promise: He did a poor job.

Crow bait: A poor-quality horse.

Shin out: To run away.

Clean someone's plow: To beat them up.

You're all down but nine: You don't understand—refers to missing all the pins in a game of nine-pin bowling.

Coffin varnish: Bad coffee.

Grub-line rider: Someone who travels from ranch to ranch looking for work.

Curly wolf: A very tough, very dangerous person.

Flannel mouth: A smooth talker.

California widow: A wife who lives apart from her husband because he has gone West to seek his fortune.

Gospel sharp: A preacher. (As skilled with the Bible as a card sharp is with cards.)

Indian haircut: A scalping.

Quirley: A cigarette you roll yourself.

Cowboy change: Bullets (sometimes used as quarters or dimes when coins were short).

Fightin' wages: Extra money paid to cowboys for fighting Indians or cattle rustlers.

Take French leave: To desert, or leave without permission.

Dude: An Easterner or well-dressed person (they wear "duds").

Someone to ride the river with: Someone dependable.

Beat the Devil around the stump: To procrastinate.

Honda: The eyelet at the end of a lasso that's used to make the loop.

"If all you have is a hammer, every problem looks like a nail." —proverb

WHO'S JUDE?

*Many pop songs were inspired by someone with personal meaning
to the songwriter. And sometimes that someone is as famous
as the person who wrote the song.*

"Uptown Girl." One of Billy Joel's biggest hits, it's an autobio-
graphical song about a blue-collar guy who falls for a girl out of his league.
Was it about Joel and his wife, supermodel Christie Brinkley, who stars in
the music video? No—he wrote it about the girlfriend he had just before
Brinkley: supermodel Elle Macpherson.

"In Your Eyes." The romantic song that John Cusack played on a hoist-
ed boombox to Ione Skye in *Say Anything* was written by singer-songwrit-
er Peter Gabriel about his then-girlfriend Rosanna Arquette. Toto's 1982
hit, "Rosanna," is also about Arquette...sort of. She was dating keyboard-
ist Steve Porcaro at the time, but singer David Paich wrote the song about
another girl; he just thought the name Rosanna sounded better in the
song.

"Hey Jude." The name Jude is a corruption of Jules, which is a nickname John Lennon gave his son Julian. Paul McCartney wrote the song
to comfort the child when his parents, John and Cynthia Lennon, were
divorcing so that Lennon could be with Yoko Ono. (Lennon later claimed
he only agreed to do the song because he thought McCartney wrote it to
comfort *him*.)

"Suicide Blonde." Michael Hutchence and Andrew Farriss of INXS
wrote this song for their 1990 album, X. At the time, Hutchence, the
biggest rock star in Australia, was dating Kylie Minogue, the biggest pop
singer in Australia. Hutchence was inspired when Minogue remarked one
day, after dying her hair platinum for a movie role, that she was going
"suicide blonde."

"Kiss Them for Me." *Kiss Them for Me* was a 1957 movie based on a play
about Navy pilots on leave in San Francisco. The film starred Cary Grant
and Jayne Mansfield, but bombed and faded into obscurity. In 1991, British alternative rock band Siouxsie and the Banshees released a song called
"Kiss Them for Me." Their biggest hit in the U.S. (and only top 30 song),

Pacific giant octopus grows from the size of a pea to 150 lbs. in 2 years...and then it dies.

the song is a meditation on Mansfield, a major movie star and sex symbol who died in a brutal car accident at the age of 34. The references to Mansfield are as obscure as the movie *Kiss Them for Me*, including Mansfield's made-up favorite word, "divoon."

"Calypso." John Denver's 1975 hit is not a tribute to Harry Belafonte, nor the island music that had a brief run of popularity in the early 1950s. No, Denver was close friends with undersea explorer and naturalist Jacques Cousteau. *Calypso* was the name of Cousteau's research vessel; the song is a tribute to him.

"Ms. Jackson." This song by rap duo Outkast went to number 1 in 2001. Directed toward the disapproving mother of an ex-girlfriend, the rappers alternate verses, expressing common feelings after a romantic split—Andre 3000's are apologetic; Big Boi's detail his anger and frustration. Andre 3000 wrote the song after breaking up with R&B singer Erykah Badu, and "Ms. Jackson" is an open letter to Badu's mother, Kolleen Gipson.

"Night Shift." Two of the most influential figures in soul music died within a few weeks of each other in 1984—Jackie Wilson, who passed away after being in a coma for eight years, and Marvin Gaye, who was murdered by his father after an argument. The Commodores, a major funk and R&B band in the '70s, wrote the song to eulogize their fallen idols, referred to by name in the song. "Night Shift" went to number 3 on the pop chart, the group's first (and only) hit after lead singer Lionel Richie left the group.

"Abraham, Martin, and John." Dick Holler became a songwriter in the late '60s after his group, the Holidays, disbanded. In 1966, he had his first big hit: the Royal Guardsmen's million-selling novelty song "Snoopy vs. the Red Baron." In 1968, after the assassination of Martin Luther King Jr., Holler wrote a more serious song—"Abraham, Martin, and John" to pay tribute to three murdered civil rights icons: Abraham Lincoln, King, and John F. Kennedy. Just as former teen idol Dion DiMucci was set to record the song, JFK's brother, Robert Kennedy, was shot—and Holler hastily wrote a verse about him. (The song went to number 4—Dion's first hit in more than five years.)

Tanzania has a postage stamp featuring Michael Jackson.

WORD ORIGINS

Ever wonder where words come from?
Here are some interesting stories.

JACKPOT
Meaning: A huge prize
Origin: "The term goes back to draw poker, where stakes are allowed to accumulate until a player is able to 'open the *pot*' by demonstrating that among the cards he has drawn he has a pair of *jacks* or better." (From *Dictionary of Word and Phrase Origins, Vol. II*, by William and Mary Morris)

GRENADE
Meaning: A small, hand-thrown missile containing an explosive
Origin: "The word comes from the French *pomegrenade*, for pomegranate, because the military missile, which dates from the sixteenth century, both is shaped like the fruit and explodes much as the seeds burst out from it." (From *Fighting Words*, by Christine Ammer)

SNACK
Meaning: A small amount of food eaten between meals
Origin: "A snack is something grabbed in a hurry, from the Dutch word *snacken*, meaning to snap at something, although that word was only used for dogs." (From *Word Origins*, by Wilfred Funk)

AMMONIA
Meaning: A potent, odorous cleaning fluid
Origin: "*Ammonia* is so called because it was first made from the dung of the worshippers' camels at the temple of Jupiter Ammon in Egypt." (From *Remarkable Words with Astonishing Origins*, by John Train)

HEATHEN
Meaning: An ungodly person
Origin: "Christianity began as primarily an urban religion; people in rural districts continued to worship older gods. The Latin word for countryman

was *paganus*—whence, of course, pagan; the Germanic tongues had a similar word, something like *khaithanaz*, 'dwelling in the heath' (wilderness)—whence heathen." (From *Loose Cannons and Red Herrings*, by Robert Claiborne)

CALCULATE

Meaning: Add, subtract, divide, and/or multiply numbers or money

Origin: "In Rome 2,000 years ago the merchant figured his profit and loss using what he called *calculi*, or 'little stones' as counters. So the Latin term *calculus*, 'pebble,' not only gave us 'calculate' but our word 'calculus,' one of the most complicated forms of modern mathematics." (From *Word Origins*, by Wilfred Funk, Litt. D.)

MUSEUM

Meaning: Building or collection of art, music, scientific tools, or any specific set of objects

Origin: A shrine to the Greek Muses. "Such a shrine was known as a *mouseion*. When the Museum at Alexandria was destroyed in the fourth century, the word nearly dropped out of use. Three hundred years ago, a scholar rediscovered the word." (From *Thereby Hangs a Tale*, by Charles Earle Funk)

DOPE

Meaning: Drugs

Origin: "This word was originally a Dutch word, *doop*, meaning a sauce or liquid. Its first association with narcotics came when it was used to describe the viscous glop that results from heating opium. Then, by rapid extension, it came to mean any narcotic." (From *Dictionary of Word and Phrase Origins, Vol. III*, by William and Mary Morris)

RIVAL

Meaning: Competitor

Origin: "A rival is etymologically 'someone who uses the same stream as another.' The word comes from Latin *rivalis*, meaning 'of a stream.' People who use or live by the same stream are neighbors and, human nature being as it is, are usually in competition with each other." (From *Dictionary of Word Origins*, by John Ayto)

Q: Why are tennis balls fuzzy? A: To slow them down.

WHAT DREAMS MEAN

Psychologists say dreams reflect our waking lives. Although translations will vary with each individual, researchers say everybody's dreams share some common themes. Here are some examples.

• **If you're naked,** you're dreading an upcoming event because you feel unprepared, ashamed, or vulnerable.

• **If you're falling,** it's a subconscious response to real-life stress. However, some experts say the "stress" could be something as simple as a mid-sleep leg or arm spasm.

• **If you die,** it doesn't portend death (yours or anybody else's)—it suggests insecurity or anxiety.

• **If you dream about a dead relative,** you've come to terms with the loss. Dream psychologists say we only dream about deceased loved ones when the grief process is complete.

• **If you see a car wreck,** a big undertaking in your life may feel bound for failure.

• **If you're being chased,** you're probably running away from something in real life. Being unable to run in a dream indicates feeling overwhelmed by daily pressures.

• **If your teeth fall out or crumble,** you're unhappy with your physical appearance. It may also mean you're excessively concerned about how others perceive you.

• **If you're giving birth,** great change is unfolding. Dreaming about babies indicates a desire to behave more maturely.

• **If you can fly,** you've just conquered a stressful situation. If you dream that you're able to control where you fly, it's a sign of confidence. Flying aimlessly suggests you're cautiously optimistic about your success.

• **If you dream about water,** it represents a general sense of your emotional state. Clear water means satisfaction with work and home. Muddy water is a sign of skepticism and discontent.

• **If you're urinating,** you may be expressing desire for relief from a difficult situation. Or you may really have to pee. Or you may be doing so already.

Role reversal: The all-male Japanese Kabuki theatre style was invented by a woman.

OUR BRIEFS ARE SHOWING

In short, we give you briefs that were too good to pass up.

JEDI TOLD YOU SO
One night in September 1955, British actor Alec Guinness (who would later play Obi-Wan Kenobi in *Star Wars*) happened to meet rising star James Dean outside of a Hollywood restaurant. Guinness invited him to dinner. "Okay," said Dean, "but first I gotta show you my new car!" Guinness followed Dean out back to a brand-new silver Porsche Spyder. "Some strange thing came over me," Guinness later recalled. "In almost a different voice than mine, I said, 'Do not get in this car.' I looked at my watch. 'It is now 10:00 on Thursday. If you get in this car, you will be found dead in it by 10:00 next Thursday.'" Dean ignored the warning. A week later, on Thursday afternoon, Dean was driving 85 mph down a California highway and collided with a truck…killing him.

AMERICA'S FAST FOOD TEST KITCHEN
After companies create new products and before they come to you, they're usually "test marketed" in a city, state, or region. This is done to test whether consumer interest is strong enough to justify a nationwide roll-out. If not, the product can be improved…or killed. Fast food companies often test market their products in Columbus, Ohio. Wendy's corporate headquarters are located there, as are the head offices of White Castle, Bob Evans, Steak Escape, and more than a dozen other chains. Panera Bread and McDonald's aren't based in Columbus, but they almost always test new products there. Why Columbus? Because demographically speaking, it's astonishingly average, making it an ideal cross-section of America. Even the median income level there is identical to the national median. Bonus: the 57,000-student Ohio State University is located in Columbus and companies are eager to make lifelong customers out of these highly impressionable—and influential—young consumers.

WHY WAS THE PIG WEARING A NECKLACE?
Posted on Craigslist in Jacksonville, Florida, in 2012: "I need help catching the gator that ate my prized pig! My pig (Rudy Belle) was wearing a very expensive necklace, a generational necklace, which was in my wife's family for years. The emotional distress I've had from losing my pig is nothing like the stress I'll receive from my wife if I don't get it back. It

"I would like to be allowed to admire a man's opinion as I would his dog—without…

happened at Blue Cypress Golf Club and it scared the bejesus out of me. If anyone has found the necklace or has seen this gator (has a weird blotchy snout), pleasssse contact me. Thanks, Jimmy T."

MYTH-INFORMATION

Myth: The famous Italian scientist Galileo Galilei (1564–1642) once released two balls from a balcony on the Leaning Tower of Pisa. With this experiment, he became the first person to show that two falling objects dropped at the same time will hit the ground at the same time, no matter how heavy or light they are.

The Truth: According to historians, there's no evidence that Galileo ever dropped anything off a tower in Pisa. The earliest account of this tall tale was written by Galileo's student and assistant, Vincenzo Viviani. Only problem: Viviani set his story decades before Galileo completed his theory on falling bodies. And even if Galileo had done the experiment, he wouldn't have been the first: Another Italian scientist, Giuseppe Moletti, had already performed the same basic experiment and reached the correct conclusion in 1576—when Galileo was only 12 years old.

YOU'RE MY INSPIRATION

In 1863 Mark Twain was a 28-year-old newspaper reporter living in San Francisco when he became friends with a local firefighter. The two men shared a passion for riverboats and talked at length about them while playing cards and drinking beer. Twain was very impressed by the young man—he'd once saved 90 people from a burning steamship. At the time, Twain was preparing to work on his first novel, which was going to be about a female firefighter called Shirley Tempest. But he scrapped that idea and instead began a book about a boy who grew up around the riverboats of the Mississippi River. The name of Twain's friend: Tom Sawyer.

STRETCHING THE TRUTH

Rubber chickens became a fad during the French Revolution (1789–1799), when soldiers dangled them from their muskets for luck. Why? It's unclear. But it doesn't matter. The French soldier story was actually spread by Loftus International, a Utah-based novelty company founded in 1939…which also happens to be the world's largest manufacturer of rubber chickens. The true origin: Somebody at Loftus came up with it. The company invented the French myth because it's more interesting (and funnier) than the truth.

FOOD A MILLENNIUM AGO

What could the average medieval peasant expect to find on the dinner table after a hard day's work? Here's the grueling tale.

I'M STARVING! WHAT'S FOR LUNCH?

For most people in the year A.D. 1000, finding enough food to eat was a constant problem. There were long periods, particularly in winter, when no fresh food was available. During the 10th century alone, Europe suffered 20 famines. As a result, people tended to gorge themselves whenever food was abundant because they never knew what the next season would bring. The staple of Joe Peasant's diet was gruel—what we'd call oatmeal—which nutritionists say was probably healthier than our modern meat-heavy diet. When vegetables were in season, people ate cabbage, carrots, peas, and various garden greens. They picked apples, pears, and nuts right off the trees.

FUNGAL FEVER

Another medieval staple was bread made from whole-grain wheat, rye, or barley flour. That may sound healthy, but unsanitary kitchens and ovens introduced other ingredients that weren't so wholesome, including insects and mold. The mold brought another problem: outbreaks of *ergotism*, a fatal illness caused by a substance called ergotamine found in a fungus that often infected rye grain. When baked into bread, the ergotamine chemically transformed into a deadly hallucinogen. Victims experienced tingling, dizziness, hallucinations, psychosis and, eventually, death. The symptoms of ergotism, according to some theories, may have caused some sufferers to be accused of witchcraft.

WOULD YOU LIKE HORSE WITH THAT?

A millennium ago, horses were just beginning to replace oxen as the quintessential farm animal. But they were still a valuable food source and were eaten with gusto. Meat was prepared with salt, pepper, cloves, and other spices, which not only preserved the food but also masked the rotten taste after it had spoiled. In addition to horses and the odd rabbit or pig, birds were eaten with regularity. People ate cranes, storks, swans, crows, herons, loons, and blackbirds, sometimes served in a pastries like the "four and twenty blackbirds baked in a pie" from the well-known English nursery rhyme.

MINIMALISM, MEDIEVAL-STYLE

Setting the medieval table was fairly simple—because there were no plates. Even nobles, who generally spread out tablecloths for their meals, went without plates. Instead, meals were served on round, flat slabs of bread. Bread plates had the dual advantages of soaking up drippings and being edible. When plates eventually came into vogue, it was customary to share your plate with the person sitting next to you.

Guests were invited to bring their own knives; spoons and forks weren't widely used in Europe until much later. In the eastern Mediterranean, two-pronged forks had been in use for centuries, but they didn't come to Europe until 1071, when a Greek princess brought the custom to Venice. Rich Venetians took it up as the fashion, but forks stayed in Venice for centuries before the rest of Europe caught on.

GROG: BREAKFAST OF CHAMPIONS

A thousand years ago, alcoholic beverages were a diversion and comfort to households among all classes. Wine was the favorite drink of the nobility and wealthier middle class. But everyone drank beer, even for breakfast, and the alcoholic content was three to four times higher than today's brews. Mead, a kind of beer made from fermented honey, was popular in northern Europe and packed an even stronger wallop—it could have an alcohol content of up to 18 percent. Beer was such a prized commodity that one Swedish king chose, among several prospective brides, the one who could brew the best beer.

* * *

FREE RANGE

Leonardo da Vinci, an avowed vegetarian, was so opposed to people eating animals that he often purchased live poultry and then set the birds free. He wrote, "I have, from an early age, abjured the use of meat, and the time will come when men such as I will look on the murder of animals as they now look on the murder of men."

NEW PRODUCTS

*Just when you think everything that could possibly
be invented has already been invented, along comes
something like rejection-letter toilet paper.*

TRUTH IN ADVERTISING

Say, what's that suspicious looking device? It's the "Suspicious Looking Device!" A darkly humorous response to the increased fears of terrorism in recent years, the SLD is a red metal box with dotted lights, a small screen, a buzzer, and whirring motor. What does it do? Nothing. It's just supposed to *appear* suspicious.

I WISH...FOR AN FTC INVESTIGATION

A company called Life Technology Research International has created the seemingly impossible: a magical wishing machine. You simply speak into the microphone on the Psychotronic Wishing Machine to tell it what you want...then sit back and wait a few days for your wish to come true. Just make sure the machine is on—LTRI says that the wish is far less likely to ever come true if the machine is turned off while the wish is still being "processed." Nevertheless, results are still *not* guaranteed. How does it work? "Conscious human interaction and energy fields." Cost: $499.

GET YOUR MOTOR RUNNIN'

For the cat owner who has everything: A California man has invented the Purr Detector. It's a small motion detector and light embedded inside a cat collar. Whenever the cat purrs, the collar glows. It's only available by mail order, so if you need to know if your cat is purring before the Purr Detector arrives, you can always use your ears.

TASTE IS NOT A FACTOR

When the gross-out game show *Fear Factor* was still on the air, it made a line of candy based on its most memorable segment: people eating disgusting animal parts. There are lollipops in the shape of a chicken's foot, pig's snout, and cow's heart (flavored lemon, bubblegum, and cinnamon, respectively) as well as candy sheep eyeballs (mango) and "coagulated

---

Cleopatra's palace in modern-day Alexandria, Egypt, is now underwater.

blood balls" (mmm…cherry!). Shockingly, the candy line is no longer available.

POT STICKERS

Many toddlers resist potty training because they're afraid of the toilet. The white porcelain behemoth is supposed to look a lot less imposing with Toilet Buddies: brightly-colored animal stickers that affix to the toilet, making it look kid-friendly enough for the little ones to use it. They're available in Poo P. Bunny, Puddles Puppy, and Ca Ca Cow.

ZOMBIE-UTIFUL

A few years ago, friends of Canadian artist Rob Sacchetto asked him to draw pictures of them as zombies to use as decorations for a Halloween party. Now Sacchetto runs a business selling Zombie Portraits. For $80, Sacchetto takes a photograph of you and uses it as the basis for a hand-drawn caricature of you as a zombie, complete with rotting flesh, oozing brains, and sagging eyeballs.

BRUSH YOUR CASTLE

Sarah Witmer had a tradition with her grandchildren: Whenever they lost a tooth, they'd put it under their pillow and the "tooth fairy" (Witmer) took it away. But this tooth fairy was a little different: A couple of days later, the kid would get a small sculpture of a castle made out of sand and the ground-up tooth. Now Witmer makes "Fairy Tooth Castles" professionally. When *your* child loses a tooth, you can send it to Witmer. She'll grind it up, mix it with sand and a hardening agent, sculpt a nine-inch-tall castle out of it, and send it back to you.

*　　　*　　　*

POOCH HOOCH

In 2013, a brewery in the beer- and dog-loving town of Bend, Oregon, released Dawg Grog, a beer brewed especially for dogs. It's made with "malted barley water, liquid glucosamine, and organic vegetable broth," but no alcohol. Cost for a 16-ounce bottle: $9. (Or you could lift the toilet seat and let Fido drink from the can.)

The first TV news helicopter was used by KTLA Channel 5 in Los Angeles, in 1958.

DIALOGUES WITH WORLD LEADERS

*Here are some unofficial exchanges involving
heads of state at official state functions.*

Queen Elizabeth II: How do you do, Mr. King?

Alan King: How do you do, Mrs. Queen?

President Nixon: You dress pretty wild, don't you?

Elvis Presley: Mr. President, you got your show to run and I got mine.

At an old folks home, President Bush approaches an old lady.

George H. W. Bush: Do you know who I am?

Old Lady: No, but if you ask in reception I'm sure they will be able to tell you.

William Gladstone: I predict, Sir, that you will die either by hanging or of some vile disease.

Benjamin Disraeli: That all depends, Sir, upon whether I embrace your principles or your mistress.

At French President Charles de Gaulle's retirement luncheon:

English guest: Madame de Gaulle, what are you looking forward to in the years ahead?

Madame de Gaulle: A penis….

…embarrassed silence…

Charles de Gaulle: My dear, I don't think the English pronounce the word like that. It is 'appiness.'

George H. W. Bush: Tell me, General, how dead is the Dead Sea?

General Zayid bin Shakr: Very dead, sir.

Woman at dinner party: You must talk to me, Mr. Coolidge. I made a bet with someone that I could get more than two words out of you.

Calvin Coolidge: You lose.

"A body of men holding themselves accountable to nobody ought not to be trusted by anybody."

—**Thomas Paine**

The rough, bumpy surface of certain types of glass (such as your shower door) is called cr

A DOTTY IDEA

*Elbert Botts's brainchild may have seemed like just a bump
in the road at the time, but it's saved countless lives.*

MEET DR. BOTTS

You may never have heard of Elbert Dysart Botts, but if you did any driving today, you probably ran over his invention. The invention? Botts Dots, the raised reflective markers seen on roads and freeways throughout the United States.

Botts didn't start out in the public-safety profession. He earned a doctorate in chemistry from the University of Wisconsin in 1924 and taught for 16 years at San Jose State University. When World War II broke out, he went to work for the government as a chemist. Then he landed a job in research and development at CalTrans (the Californian Department of Transportation), where he was assigned the task of creating a reflective paint for freeways that could be seen in heavy rain.

SPIKED

While working for CalTrans, Botts dreamed up the idea of raised markers that would alert drivers when they crossed into a different lane, avoiding unintentional lane changes and, theoretically, serious accidents. He called his innovation reflective pavement markers, or RPMs (later known by the nickname "Botts Dots"). Unfortunately, the ceramic markers cracked apart when cars rolled over them, exposing the spikes that held them to the road surface—which was bad news for tires. But one of Botts' former students came up with a solution: a durable, fast-drying epoxy that replaced the spikes. Glued-on Botts Dots have been the industry standard ever since.

FOLLOWING THE DOTTED LINE

Elbert Botts died in 1962 at age 69, a year before the first working models of his invention were installed in Northern California. Within a few years, Botts Dots were installed on roads all over the country. They've been in use ever since, and his legacy lives on every time we hear a "thump-thump-thump" when we change lanes on the freeway—or almost cross into someone else's.

stmas trees were introduced to the U.S. by Hessian troops during the Revolutionary War.

PATENTLY ABSURD

*Here's proof that the urge to invent something—anything—
is more powerful than the urge to make sure the invention
is something that people will actually want to use.*

THE INVENTION: Musical Baby Diaper Alarm
WHAT IT DOES: Three women from France marketed this alarm to mothers in 1985. It's a padded electronic napkin that goes inside a baby's diaper. When it gets wet, it plays "When the Saints Go Marching In."

THE INVENTION: The Thinking Cap
WHAT IT DOES: Improves artistic ability by mimicking the effects of autism. The cap uses magnetic pulses to inhibit the front-temporal, or "left brain" functions. This, say the two Australian scientists behind the project, creates better access to extraordinary "savant" abilities. They reported improved drawing skills in 5 of 17 volunteers in a 2002 experiment.

THE INVENTION: Pantyhose x3
WHAT IT DOES: Patented in 1997, they are three-legged panty hose. No, they're not for three-legged people, they're for women who know what it's like to get a run in their stockings. Instead of having to carry spares, you just rotate the legs. The extra leg is hidden in a pocket in the crotch; the damaged leg rolls up to take its place.

THE INVENTION: The Breath Alert
WHAT IT DOES: This pocket-sized electronic device detects and measures bad breath. You simply breathe into the sensor for three seconds, then the LCD readout indicates—on a scale of 1 to 4—how safe (or offensive) your breath is.

THE INVENTION: Weather-Reporting Toaster
WHAT IT DOES: Robin Southgate, an industrial design student at Brunel University in London, hooked up his specially made toaster to the Internet. Reading the day's meteorological stats, the toaster burns the day's predictions into a slice of bread: a sun for sunny days, a cloud with

---

Technically, you can drown without dying. "Drowning" refers to taking water into the lu

raindrops for rainy days, and so on. "It works best with white bread," says Southgate.

THE INVENTION: Separable Pants
WHAT IT DOES: You don't take them off, you take them apart. The zipper goes all the way around the crotch, from the front to the back. That way, you can mix and match the legs with other colors and styles, making your own artistic, customized pants.

THE INVENTION: Vibrating Toilet Seat
WHAT IT DOES: Thomas Bayard invented the seat in 1966. He believed that "buttocks stimulation" helps prevent constipation.

THE INVENTION: Automatic-Response Nuclear Deterrent System
WHAT IT DOES: A relic from the Cold War era, this idea was patented by British inventor Arthur Paul Pedrick in 1974. He claimed it would deter the United States, the USSR, and China from ever starting a nuclear war. How? Put three nuclear warheads on three orbiting satellites. If sensors on the satellites detected that nuclear missiles had been launched, they would automatically drop bombs: one each on Washington, Moscow, and Peking.

THE INVENTION: Lavakan
WHAT IT DOES: It's a washing machine…for cats and dogs. This industrial-strength machine soaps, rinses, and dries your pet in less than 30 minutes. One of the inventors, Andres Díaz, claims that the 5-by-5-foot, $20,000 machines can actually reduce pet stress. "One of the dogs actually fell asleep during the wash," he said. Cats weren't quite as happy about being Lavakanned. "But it's better than having a cat attach itself to your face, which is what can happen when you try to wash one by hand."

*   *   *

MILITARY INDUSTRIAL SIMPLEX

Andorra is a small country between Spain and France. In the 1970s it reported an annual defense budget of $4.90. The money was used to buy blanks to fire on national holidays.

In some parts of England, rum is used to wash a baby's head for good luck.

BRITS VS. AMERICANS:
A WORD QUIZ

People in both countries speak English, but we don't necessarily use the same words. For instance, the British call a raincoat a "mackintosh." See if you can match the British words to their American counterparts.
(Answers on page 195.)

BRITISH
1) Knackered
2) Crumpet
3) Stone
4) Nick
5) Afters
6) Rubber
7) Lollipop lady
8) Berk
9) Pilchards
10) Chuffed
11) Redundant
12) Yob
13) Brolly
14) Spot on
15) Naff
16) Dodgy
17) Nappy
18) Nutter
19) Butty
20) Plonk
21) Doddle
22) Starkers
23) Tailback
24) Wally
25) Gormless
26) Wonky
27) Ladder
28) Daps
29) Argy-bargy

AMERICAN
A) Dessert
B) Heated argument
C) Moron
D) Umbrella
E) Sandwich
F) Pleased
G) An attractive woman
H) Sneakers
I) Easy task
J) Iffy, suspect
K) Stupid
L) Exhausted
M) Run (in stockings)
N) Crossing guard
O) Worthless, unfashionable
P) Diaper
Q) Steal
R) Kook
S) Sardines
T) Cheap wine
U) Unemployed
V) Eraser
W) Perfect
X) Naked
Y) Fourteen pounds
Z) Traffic jam
AA) Nerd
BB) Unstable
CC) Hooligan

Rats were originally native to Asia. They spread throughout the world on ships.

CLOSE ENCOUNTERS OF THE CREDIBLE KIND

Investigations into 99% of UFO sightings have resulted in rational and very Earthly explanations. But then there are those few that simply have no explanation. Here are three cases that still have the experts baffled.

STRANGE BALL

In 1783 a London, England, man named Tiberius Cavallo, Fellow of the Royal Society, witnessed something that was unlike anything he'd ever seen before. "Northeast of the Terrace," he wrote in his memoirs, "in clear sky and warm weather, I saw appear suddenly an oblong cloud nearly parallel to the horizon. Below the cloud was seen a luminous body, brightly lit up and almost stationary." Cavallo described the object as a "strange ball" that was faint blue when he first saw it but then grew brighter and brighter. At one point, it flew high up into the air, then back down, and flew low across the horizon. After a few minutes, "it changed shape to oblong, acquired a tail, and seemed to split up into two bodies of small size." The object then disappeared over the horizon in a flash, and the last thing Cavallo heard from it was a "loud rumble like an explosion." Thinking the object may have crashed, Cavallo and other witnesses searched the area, but couldn't find a craft or an impact crater. One possible explanation: The "explosion" may have been a sonic boom, created when an object goes faster than the speed of sound...but this happened more than 150 years before humans had invented any type of vehicle that could break the sound barrier.

STS 48

While stationed in Earth orbit in September 1991, the Space Shuttle *Columbia*'s aft-mounted TV camera recorded video of several unidentified objects that seemed to be "swimming around." The camera was focused on an experimental tether 44 miles away, and beyond that was the horizon of the Earth. The glowing white objects intermittently entered the frame, and then turned and swam around, like microbes swimming in a petri dish. After a few minutes, a white flash appeared in the bottom left corner of the screen and suddenly, as if on cue, the little white objects all turned in unison and zoomed out of the frame. A few seconds later, a streak of light entered the frame and seemed to pause. Then, inexplicably, the camera rotated down toward the cargo bay, which was completely out of focus, then rotated back up…and the lights were gone.

NASA has dismissed the objects as "normal ice and debris" that sometimes float around ships in orbit. But these weren't floating; they were moving independently of each other and changing direction. And the occasional "debris" NASA referred to is usually found close to the ship. The camera was focused miles away on the long tether, and some of the objects appeared to fly *behind* the tether. So what were these things? No one knows for sure. They are truly unidentified flying objects.

FLAMING ARROW

On the night of June 30, 2002, a UFO was sighted across nearly all of central China. It was first seen over the eastern province of Jiangsu, then moved west, over Henan province, then Xiaxi province, and then Sichuan. "At 10:30 p.m., an object resembling a flaming arrow appeared in the night sky," wrote Henan's *City Morning Post* the next day. "Then the tail of the fiery arrow opened up like a fan, which emitted bright light. The light-emitting section then changed into a crescent. A fireball on top of the crescent glowed brilliantly. Five minutes later, the UFO disappeared."

Dozens of other newspapers reported the event, based on thousands of eyewitness accounts. The government had no explanation, except to say that it was definitely not a Chinese craft. Wang Sichao, a well-respected astronomer at Nanjing's Zijinshan Astronomy Center, studied the reports and photographs, and offered this conclusion: "It is a dimensional flying machine. But whether it is of human origin or extraterrestrial, whether it is controlled inside or remotely, are still unknown. Maybe we will not be able to uncover the truth for many years, but human curiosity will never let us stop searching."

Hailey Jo Bauer was born on August 8, 2008 (8/8/08) at 8:08 a.m. She weighed 8 lb., 8

THE LEAGUE OF COMIC BOOK CREATORS

By day, they were mild-mannered writers and artists. But at night…well, they stayed mild-mannered writers and artists, but they also thought up some of the most popular comic book characters the world has ever known. Come meet the men behind the Man of Steel, the Dark Knight, and the mutants.

SUPERMAN: Joe Schuster & Jerry Siegel

Schuster & Siegel created *Superman* in 1936, when the Cleveland duo (Siegel born there, and Schuster having moved there at age nine from Toronto) tried selling the Man of Steel as a comic strip to the newspapers. No one bought it until 1938, when DC Comics gave *Superman* a tryout in its Action Comics book. The rest is history, and Schuster & Siegel would go on to fame and fortune, right? Not exactly. By contract, DC Comics retained all rights in the Superman character, and so while the publishing company was making millions from *Superman*, Schuster & Siegel were not. They weren't doing poorly—in 1940 *The Saturday Evening Post* noted that the two of them were making $75,000 a year between them—but they knew they could be doing much better.

They sued DC Comics in 1946, and in 1948 received a relatively small settlement (a reported $120,000). But the flip side of the settlement was that the duo's byline, previously on every *Superman* story, was removed from all future products. Schuster soon left the comic book field, and Siegel's work slowed to a trickle. In the 1970s, while Hollywood geared up for the *Superman* movie starring Christopher Reeve, Schuster & Siegel again got the word out about how badly they had been treated by DC and sued the company once more. Although the courts decided the writers didn't have a case, DC was pressured by the comic book community into providing both men with a $35,000-per-year stipend for as long as they lived. Schuster died in 1992; Siegel passed away in 1996.

BATMAN: Bob Kane

Like Schuster & Siegel, Kane handed over his comic book creation, *Batman*, to DC Comics, where the Caped Crusader made his first appearance in

1939. However, unlike Superman's creators, Kane maintained a small percentage of the take every time the cash register rang up a Batman sale. How did he do it? He had a lawyer in the family, who advised him to retain his copyright interests.

Keeping a stake in the Dark Knight did good things for Kane's income and his leisure time. Although his name was kept on all the Batman stories, he handed off most of the work to underlings in what was one of the biggest open secrets in comics. Kane himself headed to Hollywood to create animated TV shows (such as *Courageous Cat*) and to advise in the development of the campy 1960s *Batman* TV series. He even had a cameo in 1997's *Batman and Robin*, as did his wife. Kane died in 1998.

THE X-MEN & THE INCREDIBLE HULK: Jack Kirby

Kirby, who started working in comics in 1938, was arguably the most prolific comic book character creator around. Characters he created or co-created include the X-Men, the Incredible Hulk, and the Fantastic Four, as well as Captain America, Iron Man, the Silver Surfer, and Thor (the last one with a little help from Norse mythology). Some comic fans also give him a shared credit (along with DC's Stan Lee) for Spider-Man. Most of Kirby's greatest creations are associated with Marvel Comics, but he worked off and on for a number of comic book publishers, including DC; he bounced between the two majors for much of his career.

Kirby was also not above doing grunt work. In the mid-1950s, when worries about the morality of comic books caused the industry to collapse and the superhero genre was gutted (350 comic book titles stopped publication), Kirby stayed in business by drawing romance comics. His artistic output throughout his career was staggering—more than 24,000 pages of comic book art. In 1994, at the age of 76, Kirby died at his home in California.

*   *   *

"The right answer to a fool is silence."

—Afghani proverb

In Old Testament times, the Mediterranean Sea was called the Great Sea.

OFFICE ORIGINS

The stories behind the stuff you use at work every day.

THE COMPUTER MOUSE

In the 1960s, computers still operated by having users enter long lines of code, which could be why they were used primarily at academic and research facilities. A Stanford Research Institute engineer named Douglas Engelbart thought computers would be a lot easier to use if they were more interactive. While sitting in a meeting one day, he thought about creating a small wheeled object that would move across a table, and its movements would translate to moving a cursor across the screen. He wasn't the first to come up with the idea, but he and fellow engineer Bill English incorporated technology from some other SRI prototypes into his design (including a foot-pedaled cursor controller) and created a handheld wooden box with two wheels on the bottom and a button on the top. After writing software that made the computer able to recognize the device, they wired it into the computer, and as Engelbart wheeled the box around his desk, the cursor on his screen moved accordingly. Engelbart patented it as an "X/Y Position Indicator," but his coworkers thought it looked like a mouse. So that became its name.

BINDER CLIPS

In the early 20th century, here's how you bundled a large stack of papers together: punch holes into the left side of each sheet, thread twine between the holes, and bind them together like a book. It was secure, but annoying if you had to remove a page. You'd have to unthread the stack, remove the page, and then rethread it. Sixteen-year-old Louis Baltzley saw his father—an inventor who often had to revise patent applications—do it hundreds of times. In 1911, he had an idea. Inspired by surgical clamps, he made a hinged metal clamp. It could bind a stack of pages, but if one had to be removed, he simply opened the clamp. More than 100 years later, the design of the binder clip is largely unchanged.

The Wright Brothers tested their first airplane in a wind tunnel before flying it.

PHOTOCOPIERS

Chester Carlson graduated with a physics degree in 1930—at the beginning of the Great Depression. Jobs were scarce then, and the only work he could find was as a clerk in the patent department of Bell Labs in New York. The job—hand-copying patent applications, along with their included sketches and charts—exacerbated the arthritis in his hands, so Carlson set out to create an automatic document-copying technique.

He set up shop on his kitchen table in Queens and started experimenting with *photoconductivity*, charging metal plates with static electricity to make chemical powders cling to the plate and then applying heat (from his stove) to transfer an image to paper. In 1938, Carlson made a glass slide with the date on it, rubbed cotton against a sulfur-coated zinc plate, and then pressed the slide to the plate. He held the slide up to a light, dusted it with chemical powders, then pressed the slide to paper on the heated plate. The image transferred. In 1945, after GE and IBM turned it down, the Haloid Company bought Carlson's technology. They called the process xerography, Greek for "dry writing," and named the machine that performed it a Xerox. Xerox machines sold moderately in the 1950s, but sales soared when the first fully automated push-button model was introduced in 1960. By 1968, the Xerox Corporation was selling $1 billion worth of copiers a year.

LASER PRINTERS

After Xerox debuted the photocopier, a Xerox employee named Gary Starkweather wondered if the technology could be used to print documents directly from the company's mainframe computer. He worked for two years, from 1967 to 1969, modifying a Xerox copier, replacing its photographic machinery with a mirrored eight-sided drum and a laser. The laser's light bounced off the spinning drum, burning images onto the paper as it moved through the machine. Starkweather had invented what he called the Scanned Laser Output Terminal (SLOT), but it was used only internally at Xerox until 1977. That year, the company debuted the Xerox 9700 laser printer commercially. It's now the standard method of printing in offices (and homes) around the world.

Southern Florida is the only place where alligators and crocodiles both live.

I'D LIKE TO THANK THE ACADEMY...

Every year, Hollywood puts on the movie industry's biggest party. But there's more to the Academy Awards than sealed envelopes, gold statues, and acceptance speeches. Here are a few little-known facts about the Oscars.

An **Oscar isn't really called an "Oscar."** It's not even officially called an Academy Award. The award's full title is the Academy Award of Merit. The "Academy" refers to the Academy of Motion Pictures Arts and Sciences, formed in 1927 by film-industry employees to arbitrate labor disputes, provide a forum for teaching movie-making techniques and innovations, and improve the industry's image. In 1929, almost as an afterthought, it began giving out awards for achievement. Most people now associate the Academy only with the awards, but it also continues its other functions (except that it ended its involvement with labor disputes in 1937).

• **At the first ceremony, only 14 awards were given out.** The original award categories were: Actor, Actress, Art Direction, Cinematography, Directing (Comedy), Directing (Drama), Engineering Effects, Unique and Artistic Picture, Writing (Adaptation), Writing (Original), Writing (Title Writing), Outstanding Picture (which went to *Wings*), and two "special achievement" awards. The ceremony lasted 15 minutes; admission was $5.

• **The winners' names were not always closely guarded secrets.** The 1929 ceremony was an unpretentious dinner in the Blossom Room of the Hollywood Roosevelt Hotel. Everyone already knew who had won; the results had been announced nearly three months earlier. The following year, the Academy gave the press the names of the winners ahead of time—on the condition that they wouldn't print the results until after the ceremony. That tradition continued until 1939 when, during a heated race for Best Picture among heavyweight contenders such as *Stagecoach*, *The Wizard of Oz*, *Gone With the Wind*, and *Mr. Smith Goes to Washington*, the *Los Angeles Times* printed the name of the winner (*Gone With the Wind*) in its early evening edition—a few hours before the ceremony, ruining the suspense. Since then, the winners are revealed *only* at the ceremony.

Something missing? The Mona Lisa is *epalperbate*—without eyebrows.

CASTLE IN THE DESERT

*How a cowboy named "Death Valley Scotty" conned his way into
fame, fortune…and a big house that didn't belong to him.*

HOT PROPERTY

In a desolate canyon in Death Valley National Park sits a
33,000-square-foot Spanish-Mediterranean castle with 14
bathrooms, 14 fireplaces, 4 kitchens, a solar water heating plant, a hydro-
electric generating system, a gas station, stables for dozens of horses, and a
56-foot clock tower complete with 25 chimes. The main house has a rock
wall fountain, is decorated with European antiques, hand-painted tiles,
and handcrafted ironwork, and features a theater organ with 1,121 pipes
and a 250-foot unfinished swimming pool. The castle sits on 1,500 acres
and is surrounded by a 45-mile-long fence. It cost $2 million to build in
the 1920s.

Walter Scott lived there in high style for decades. He claimed the
castle as his own and said that it sat atop a gold mine. But the truth was
he didn't have a cent.

A DRIFTING GRIFTER

Walter Scott was born in Kentucky in 1872. He left home at 11 to
become a cowboy in Nevada and, at 13, got a job working as a water boy
for the Harmony Borax Works in Death Valley. By the time he was 18,
he was such a skilled rider that Buffalo Bill Cody offered Scott a role in
his Wild West Show. For 12 years Scott traveled and performed throughout the United States and Europe. In 1901 he arrived in New York City,
where he was supposed to ride into town with the other performers. But
he went out drinking instead. Buffalo Bill saw Scott standing drunk (and
cheering) along the parade route and fired him on the spot.

He was out of work but not out of ideas. Scott had (unsuccessfully)
worked a gold mine for one winter in Colorado, so, well versed in the art
of publicity from his days with the Wild West Show, he invented a tale
about a gold mine in Death Valley, one of the most remote areas of the
country and the perfect place to hide a fictitious gold mine. Scott lured
several New York investors with tales of the lucrative mine and

---

"I never knew an early-rising, hard-working, prudent man, careful of his earnings, and

convinced them to give him money to excavate the ore in exchange for a percentage of the profits.

A PRO AT CONS

There was no mine, but Scott took the money anyway and headed to California. Once there, he lived it up in the towns around Death Valley and in Los Angeles. He stayed in expensive hotels and tipped in large bills.

Even though none of the money went to mining equipment, he continued spinning his tale and investors continued to give him money. When his backers asked why they hadn't seen any ore or profits from the mine, Scott put them off, saying there had been a mule stampede, a flash flood, or a run-in with bandits.

ENTER ALBERT JOHNSON

One investor, though, started to distrust Scott's excuses. Born in 1872, Albert Johnson had made a fortune in zinc mining but also made several bad investments. In 1906 Johnson invested in Scott's gold mine.

Three years passed before Johnson began to doubt Scott's tales, but in 1909, he traveled to California to see for himself the Death Valley Mine whose riches never seemed to materialize. Scott agreed to take Johnson to the mine, believing the trip would prove too difficult for the Easterner and that Johnson would back out before they ever reached the "site." But Johnson loved the desert. Ten years earlier, he'd been injured in a train crash, and he still suffered the ill effects of a broken back. The dry climate and the adventure in Death Valley made him feel better than he had in years.

It didn't take long for Johnson to realize there was no mine, but he had such a good time in Death Valley that he didn't care that he'd been duped. He kept returning to the area and eventually bought 1,500 acres in Grapevine Canyon. When his wife, Bessie, began accompanying him on his trips and grew tired of the tents and rude shack that served as accommodations, Johnson decided to build a permanent home.

HOME ON THE RANGE

In 1925 Albert Johnson approached Frank Lloyd Wright to design a house, to be called the "Death Valley Ranch." But Wright's design wasn't grand enough for Johnson, so he hired a second architect, C. Alexander

MacNeiledge. Over the next five years, the castle started to take shape. And because the home was so elaborate, its construction revived the rumors of Scott's gold strike, rumors that neither Scott nor Johnson did anything to quiet. In fact, Scott (who by this time had earned the nickname "Death Valley Scotty") bragged to reporters about the castle and said it belonged to him. Johnson perpetuated the lie and would say only that he was "Scotty's banker." So Death Valley Ranch became known as "Scotty's Castle."

In 1931 construction on the castle stopped. The 1929 stock market crash had cost Johnson most of his fortune, and he could no longer afford to keep building. The castle stood unfinished.

DEATH (VALLEY) AND TAXES

In the early 1930s, the federal government began surveying Death Valley in preparation for making it a national monument and discovered that Albert Johnson didn't actually own the land on which he'd built the castle—the boundary for Johnson's land was one mile away. It took four years for Johnson to get permission from the government, but in 1937, he bought the land he thought he already owned for $1.25 an acre.

Death Valley officially became a national monument in 1933 and the tourists began pouring in. Johnson, still needing money, opened up the castle for guided tours and paying guests. He and his wife moved to a house in Los Angeles, but Scotty remained at the castle, where he entertained visitors with jokes and stories of the Wild West.

Scotty also continued to brag about the gold mine, which brought some unwelcome attention in the early 1940s. The Internal Revenue Service wanted to know why Scotty had never paid any income taxes on this supposedly fabulous wealth. Finally, Albert Johnson had to admit that he owned the castle and Scott never had a gold mine in Death Valley.

END OF AN ERA

Albert Johnson died in 1948, but Death Valley Scotty lived at the ranch until his death in 1954. After that, a charitable organization called the Gospel Foundation inherited the castle and maintained it. In 1970 the National Park Service bought the site for $850,000.

Today, 200,000 people visit the ranch annually. Park officials wear authentic 1930s garb and regale tourists with the tale of Death Valley Scotty and the legend he built on a lie.

THE BUGS AND THE BEES

We sometimes wonder about insects creeping and crawling
in the garage or out in the garden. What do they do all
day? It turns out that even with six or eight legs,
they still have a one-track mind.

CHEAPSKATE FLIES

The mating ritual of a type of fly called *Hilara*, commonly known as the "dance fly," involves gift-giving. The male catches a small insect, wraps it in silk, and then presents it—along with a wing-waving mating dance—to his potential mate. When she accepts it, he mounts her while she's busy eating the gift. But some dance flies are too lazy to even catch the bug. In one species, the male offers the female what *looks* like a gift-wrapped insect. While she unwraps it, he mates with her, trying to complete the act before she discovers there's no bug in the bag.

TRICKY ORCHIDS

The female tiphiid wasp can't fly. So she climbs to the top of a tall plant and releases her pheromones into the air. The male flies by, grabs her, and flies away. Mating takes place in midair.

One type of orchid has made an interesting adaptation: its flower looks just like a female tiphiid. Not only that, its scent is almost identical to her pheromones. The unsuspecting male wasp grabs the flower and tries to take off with it; in the struggle, he brushes against the pollen before becoming frustrated and flying away. He goes on to the next orchid and goes through the same routine, thus pollinating the orchids.

HUNGRY SPIDERS

The female black widow spider is genetically programmed to control the black widow population in her neighborhood, based on available food supply. Here's how she does it: A male approaches her web, sits on the edge, and bobs his abdomen, causing the web to vibrate. If she's not in the mood, she won't respond. If she is willing to mate, she'll send out an answering pattern of vibrations calling him toward her. But if she's hungry, she'll send the male the *exact same* mating response. And when he gets close enough… she eats him.

A 30-second commercial costs about as much to produce as a 30-minute sitcom.

ODD SUPERHEROES

*But are they really any odder than a guy who wears his red underwear
over his blue tights or a guy who shoots goo out of his wrists?*

BOUNCING BOY. First appearing in a 1961 Action comic, Chuck
Taine drank what he thought was a bottle of soda, but it was really
a "super-plastic fluid" that gives him the ability to turn into a
gigantic bouncing ball. He even gets to join the Legion of Superheroes
(sidekicks of Superboy) along with other uniquely powered characters,
such as Matter-Eater Lad (his superpower: He can eat anything).

ZSAZSA ZATURNNAH. By day, Ada is the meek owner of a beauty
salon in a small town in the Philippines (where the comic originates). At
night, he eats a piece of magic rock and transforms himself into Zsazsa, a
muscular, curvaceous, crime-fighting woman.

SUPER PRESIDENT. On this 1967 cartoon show, American President
James Norcross gets caught in a "cosmic storm" and gains the ability to
turn himself into steel, water, stone, or electricity.

SUPERDUPONT. Satirizing French stereotypes, this 1972 French-
made superhero is a snooty, mustachioed Frenchman who wears a beret,
carries a baguette, drinks red wine, and smokes Gauloise cigarettes.
He flies around foiling the schemes of an enemy organization called
"Anti-France."

LEECH. His parents abandoned him at birth because he had green skin
and hollow eyes. Even his superhero friends (Leech is a minor character
in *X-Men* comics) avoid him because his power is to negate the powers of
those around him.

AQUANUS. An Indonesian version of Aquaman, he can breathe underwater and communicate with fish. But he can do something Aquaman
can't—he can shoot rainbows from his belt.

GENERATION TESLA. In this 1995 Serbian comic, inventor Nikola
Tesla transports himself to another dimension and reanimates a bunch of
dead people and gives them all superpowers.

Crazy fact: About one in four U.S. adults will suffer from a diagnosable mental disorder thi

STAGE NAME STORIES

Would these celebrities have become famous if they'd stuck with their birth names?
We'll never know, but here's how they got the names we know them by.

DANA ELAINE OWENS. When this future rap star, singer, and actress was eight years old in 1978, her cousin, who was Muslim, told her the Arabic word for "gentle and kind" is *latifah*. "I really felt like that name fit me," she said. At 17, she needed a new first name for her rap moniker: "I chose 'Queen' because my mother told me that all women were queens and should be treated as such," which is how she became Queen Latifah.

JOAN ALEXANDRA MOLINSKY. While attending college in the mid-1950s, the comedienne called herself "J. Sondra Meredith," mostly to distance herself from the surname of her disapproving parents, who thought that female comics were "as bad as showgirls." The owner of the first comedy club didn't like "Meredith" and called her "Pepper January," but she hated that. When she finally got an agent, Tony Rivers, he told her, "I can't send you out with *that* name." So she chose his, and became Joan Rivers.

MAURICE JOSEPH MICKLEWHITE. Born in London in 1933, Micklewhite got his first job in theater at age 20. Disliking both his first and last names, he billed himself as Michael Scott. But in 1954, while standing in a London phone booth talking to his agent, he was informed there already was an English actor named Michael Scott. Pressured to choose a new name right there, Micklewhite looked down the street and saw a movie marquee sign advertising *The Caine Mutiny*. So he said to his agent, "Michael Caine."

JEROME SILBERMAN. One of the biggest names in comedy started out as a serious dramatic actor. But he couldn't imagine seeing "Jerry Silberman as Hamlet" on a playbill, so in 1959, when he was 26 years old, he chose a new name by combining Eugene Gant, a character in Thomas Wolfe's novel *Look Homeward, Angel*, with playwright Thornton Wilder. Later in his life, the *Willy Wonka* actor joked, "I can't imagine Gene Wilder playing Hamlet, either."

Rabbits are more closely related to horses than to rodents.

MICHAEL JOHN DOUGLAS. When this young comedian left Pittsburgh in the early 1970s (after a brief stint as one of the "Flying Zookeeni Brothers" on *Mister Rogers' Neighborhood*), he had trouble making a name for himself in Hollywood because there were already two famous Michael Douglases (an actor and a talk-show host). Legend has it that he chose his new surname because of a crush on actress Diane Keaton, but Michael Keaton actually got it from one of his all-time favorite funnymen, silent-film star Buster Keaton.

DESTINY HOPE CYRUS. Born in 1992—the year her father Billy Ray Cyrus achieved worldwide fame with the country song "Achy Breaky Heart"—the baby girl had such a sunny disposition that she was nicknamed "Smiley," later shortened to Miley. To honor her dad, she legally changed her name to Miley Ray Cyrus.

NATALIE HERSHLAG. She chose her stage name at age 13 when she landed her first movie role in 1994's *The Professional.* It's not because Hershlag isn't "Hollywood" enough—rather, she wanted her family's privacy protected if she ever became famous. She chose her grandmother's maiden name and is professionally known as Natalie Portman.

ERIC MARLON BISHOP. In 1989, this Texas comic was having trouble getting called up on stage at open-mic nights. Noticing that there were a dozen male comics for every female comic—and the ladies were getting called up first—Bishop wrote a more feminine-sounding name on the sign-up sheet to fool the emcee. It worked: As "Jamie Foxx," he *was* called up to perform. (The last name was in honor of comedian Red Foxx.) "A stage name is like having a Superman complex," Foxx once told Oprah Winfrey, "I go into the telephone booth as Eric Bishop and come out as Jamie Foxx."

JONATHAN STUART LEIBOWITZ. Talk-show host Jon Stewart has given several explanations as to why he dropped his last name: It was too hard to pronounce, kids in middle school called him "Leiboshitz," and "Leibowitz just sounded too Hollywood." But in truth, he'd been uncomfortable with his name ever since 1971, when his father, physicist Donald Leibowitz, divorced his mother. In 1987, after a New York comedy club emcee butchered his name, he decided then and there to leave the name "Leibowitz" behind.

The average married Englishwoman living in the 1600s gave birth to 13 children.

I TOAST YOU!

On a recent trip to Ireland, Uncle John spent many an evening going from pub to pub collecting traditional toasts (and many a morning after, begging for aspirin). Here are some favorites.

May you have food and clothing, a soft pillow for your head; May you be forty years in heaven, before the devil knows you're dead.

For every wound, a balm. For every sorrow, a cheer. For every storm, a calm. For every thirst, a beer.

May the roof above us never fall in, and may we friends gathered below never fall out.

Here's health and prosperity, to you and all your posterity, And them that doesn't drink with sincerity, That they may be damned for all eternity!

Gentlemen, start your livers!

May we live to learn well, and learn to live well.

May your right hand always be stretched out in friendship and never in want.

Here's to warm words on a cold evening, A full moon on a dark night, And the road downhill all the way to your door.

Success to the lover, honor to the brave, health to the sick, and freedom to the slave.

May the Lord keep you in His hand, And never close His fist too tight on you.

Old wood to burn, old books to read, old wine to drink, old friends to trust.

May misfortune follow you the rest of your life, but never catch up.

Champagne to our real friends, and real pain to our sham friends.

May you live as long as you want, and never want as long as you live.

May I see you gray, combing your grandchildren's hair.

May the people who dance on your grave get cramps in their legs.

Health and long life to you, The woman of your choice to you, A child every year to you, Land without rent to you, And may you die in Ireland.

The point where your nose meets your forehead is called the *nasion*.

THAT'S ABOUT THE SIZE OF IT

Most people never give a second thought to life's most important questions, such as: How tall should a bowling pin be? Fortunately for them, Uncle John does. Here's a look at the standard sizes of everyday objects.

Soccer Ball: Must measure between 27 and 28 inches in circumference and weigh 14 to 16 ounces.

Napkin (dinner): Should be no less than 183 square inches, unfolded. (A cocktail napkin should be no larger than 100 square inches, unfolded.)

Boulder: An "official" boulder must be at least 256 millimeters (10.07 inches) in diameter.

Pebble: A pebble must be no smaller than 4 millimeters (0.16 inch) and no larger than 64 millimeters (2.51 inches) in diameter.

Bowling ball: Should be 27 inches in circumference and weigh no more than 16 pounds.

Bowling pin: Should weigh between 3 pounds, 2 ounces and 3 pounds, 10 ounces and should be exactly 1 foot, 3 inches tall.

Dart: Cannot be more than 1 foot in length, or weigh more than 50 grams.

Dartboard: Must be hung so that the bull's-eye is 5 feet, 8 inches above the floor. The person throwing the dart must stand 7 feet, 9 $\frac{1}{4}$ inches from the board.

Wash cloth: Should be a square of cloth no smaller than 12 by 12 inches and no larger than 14 by 14 inches.

Compact car: Must weigh at least 3,000 pounds, but no more than 3,500.

Parachute: To slow a 200-pound person to a landing speed of 20 feet per second, a parachute must be 28 feet in diameter.

Golf ball: Must weigh no more than 1.62 ounces, with a diameter no less than 1.68 inches. (A standard tee is 2 $\frac{1}{8}$ inches long.)

King mattress: Must be no smaller than 80 inches long and 76 inches wide.

Jumbo egg: One dozen jumbo eggs should weigh no less than 30 ounces.

No plant on Earth has an absolutely black blossom.

LOVE AT FIRST SIGHT?

*Uncle John actually fell in love at first sight. So smooth
and shiny. Those perfect proportions. That beautiful
white…porcelain. You thought we were talking
about Mrs. Uncle John? Oh, yeah. Her too.*

HERE'S LOOKING AT YOU

You're looking around a crowded room, and your eyes meet the eyes of another. Pow! A shock runs through your whole body! Are you in love? Maybe. Read on to find out. That jolt isn't imaginary. Scientists say that part of your brain actually perks up when you exchange looks with a person you consider attractive.

And just how did they discover that? British researchers used a special helmet to scan the brains of 16 volunteers (8 men and 8 women). Wearing an fMRI (functional magnetic resonance imaging) helmet, each volunteer looked at 160 photos of 40 complete strangers.

In some photos, the strangers were looking directly at the camera— which made them appear to be looking directly at the volunteer. In others, the stranger's eyes were turned away.

As the photos went flashing by—one every 3.5 seconds—the helmets recorded which part of the volunteer's brain was active. After the brain scan was finished, the volunteers went back to the pictures and rated each one for attractiveness. The results of the experiment were published in 2001 in *Nature* magazine.

REAL SPARKS

Every time a volunteer saw an attractive person looking right at them, the volunteer's ventral striatum lit up—that part of the brain is linked to the anticipation of a reward. But when the stranger in the photo was looking away, the magic didn't happen; there was much less brain activity, no matter how attractive the person in the photo. The researchers attributed that to disappointment—the volunteer had failed to make eye contact with an attractive face.

The brain response happened fast—in just nanoseconds. Researchers think this means that it's automatic, that we're all wired for that kind of reaction.

EYES OF THE BEHOLDER

Does this mean that everybody responds to certain kinds of looks? The leading researcher, Dr. Knut Kampe of the Institute of Cognitive Neuroscience in London, commented that we all might naturally respond to people who look strong and healthy. That could be connected with survival. But Kampe said that each of the volunteers defined attractiveness in different ways, and conventional beauty wasn't the only important thing. Some looked for cheerfulness, others for a face that seemed to show empathy. Some even looked for motherliness.

IS IT LOVE?

So does it mean that love at first sight is real? Can we expect to instantly recognize our perfect mate? Probably not. Consider the following:

• Seeing a certain someone can get your brain buzzing—but so can seeing food when you're hungry. The ventral striatum that responded to the photos is the same area that lights up in hungry lab animals who think they're about to get fed. Gamblers and drug addicts have the same kind of reaction to the objects of their desire. That part of your brain gets excited when it expects *any* kind of reward.

• The brain's quick response helps explain why we make snap judgments about people we meet. But first impressions can be wrong.

• The same brain area lit up for any attractive face—no matter whether it was the opposite sex or the same sex as the volunteer. Researchers think that's because attractiveness often gets associated with social status. So maybe your brain assumes that hanging out with attractive people could improve your position. (In the case of monkeys, bonding with an animal higher up in the pecking order brings increased social status.)

So if you're expecting a future with someone based on the jolt you got when your eyes met—slow down. You'll have to engage some other part of your brain to find out whether the two of you actually get along.

*   *   *

A SHOWER OF STATS

According to surveys, 57% of Americans shower daily, 17% sing in the shower, 4% shower with the lights off, and 3% clean their pets by showering with them.

Some asteroids have other asteroids orbiting them.

FINAL THOUGHTS

If you had to pick some last words, what would they be?
Here are a dozen that people are still quoting.

"Don't worry—it's not loaded."
    —**Terry Kath, leader of the band Chicago, playing Russian roulette**

"I should never have switched from Scotch to Martinis."
    —**Humphrey Bogart**

"How about this for a headline for tomorrow's paper? French fries."
    —**James French, executed in the Oklahoma electric chair, 1966**

"I'll take a wee drop of that. I don't think there's much fear of me learning to drink now."
    —**Dr. James Cross, Scottish physicist and lifelong teetotaler**

"Am I dying, or is this my birthday?"
    —**Lady Astor, awaking to find her relatives gathered around her bedside**

"And now, I am officially dead."
    —**Abram S. Hewitt, industrialist, after removing the oxygen tube from his mouth**

"I've had 18 straight whiskeys. I think that's the record!"
    —**Dylan Thomas, poet**

"Why, of course….That's His line of work."
    —**Heinrich Heine, German poet, on being told that God would forgive his sins**

"So little done. So much to do!"
    —**Alexander Graham Bell**

"I desire to go to hell and not to heaven. In the former place I shall enjoy the company of popes, kings, and princes, while the latter are only beggars, monks and apostles."
    —**Niccolo Machiavelli**

"Waiting, are they? Waiting, are they? Well, let 'em wait."
    —**General Ethan Allen, Revolutionary War hero, on being told, "The angels are waiting for you."**

"Either the wallpaper goes, or I do."
    —**Oscar Wilde**

There are more pets per person in France than in any other country in the world.

ANSWER PAGES

PLOP, PLOP, QUIZ, QUIZ

(Answers for page 50)

1) **E.** Maxwell House coffee
2) **J.** Allstate insurance
3) **B.** Perdue chickens
4) **G.** Brylcreem
5) **F.** Federal Express
6) **I.** Schlitz beer
7) **N.** Hebrew National hot dogs
8) **L.** Alka-Seltzer
9) **D.** Morton's salt
10) **A.** American Express
11) **C.** Packard
12) **M.** Remington shavers
13) **H.** Timex
14) **K.** AT&T

PLOP, PLOP, QUIZ, QUIZ TWO

(Answers for page 65)

1) **G.** Yellow Pages
2) **K.** Energizer batteries
3) **D.** Marlboro cigarettes
4) **J.** Bactine ointment
5) **H.** Milk
6) **B.** Cattlemen's Beef Board
7) **L.** Delta Airlines
8) **M.** Bartles & Jaymes wine coolers
9) **N.** Chrysler Cordoba
10) **I.** General Foods International Coffees
11) **F.** Irish Spring soap
12) **E.** Pepsi
13) **A.** Motel 6
14) **C.** DuPont

NOVEL STARTS
(Answers for pages 153–154)

1. *Roots*
2. *The Old Man and the Sea*
3. *The Secret Garden*
4. *Atlas Shrugged*
5. *Fahrenheit 451*
6. *Frankenstein*
7. *The Adventures of Tom Sawyer*
8. *1984*
9. *Metamorphosis*
10. *Moby Dick*
11. *David Copperfield*
12. *The Call of the Wild*
13. *Wuthering Heights*
14. *War and Peace*
15. *Rebecca*
16. *The Great Gatsby*
17. *The Red Badge of Courage*
18. *Dracula*
19. *The Color Purple*
20. *Pride and Prejudice*

The Mason-Dixon line had nothing to do with slavery. It was surveyed in 1767...

BRITS VS. AMERICANS: A WORD QUIZ

(Answers for page 174)

1) **L.** Exhausted
2) **G.** An attractive woman
3) **Y.** Fourteen pounds
4) **Q.** Steal
5) **A.** Dessert
6) **V.** Eraser
7) **N.** Crossing guard
8) **C.** Moron
9) **S.** Sardines
10) **F.** Pleased

11) **U.** Unemployed
12) **CC.** Hooligan
13) **D.** Umbrella
14) **W.** Perfect
15) **O.** Worthless, unfashionable
16) **J.** Iffy, suspect
17) **P.** Diaper
18) **R.** Kook
19) **E.** Sandwich
20) **T.** Cheap wine

21) **I.** Easy task
22) **X.** Naked
23) **Z.** Traffic jam
24) **AA.** Nerd
25) **K.** Stupid
26) **BB.** Unstable
27) **M.** Run (in stockings)
28) **H.** Sneakers
29) **B.** Heated argument

OL' JAY'S BRAINTEASERS

(Answers for page 54)

1. **BRIGHT THINKING**: Standing in the hallway, Amy turned on the first light switch. She waited two minutes and then turned on the second light switch. Then after another minute she turned them both off. When she walked into the library, one was very hot, the other was slightly warm, and the other was cold—making it easy for her to tell Uncle John which switch turned on which lamp.

2. **MYSTERY JOB**: Brian works at a library.

3. **SIDE TO SIDE**: The river was frozen.

4. **SPECIAL NUMBER**: *8,549,176,320*
When spelled out, it contains each number—zero through nine—in alphabetical order.

5. **TIME PIECES**: An hourglass. It is filled with thousands of grains of sand.

6. **WORD PLAY**: If you remove the first letter of each word and place it on the end of the word, it will spell the same word backwards.

...to settle a border dispute between British colonies.

THE JOY OF SECTS
(Answers for page 122)

1. A or C. Bravo if you eliminated Quakers and Moravians right away—they don't wear old-fashioned clothes. As for the other two, take another look at the clothes. Color doesn't matter, but patterns do. The Amish wear only solid colors, so anything else suggests the girls are Mennonites.

2. D. Amish communities do not have churches. Instead, they hold Sunday services in different homes each week, so a wagon-load of benches is delivered to the designated house. Most Amish homes have dark green window shades. Why the plain, identical window treatments? The Amish community would consider decorative shades or frilly curtains signs of vanity.

3. B. Although a basket of buns and mugs of coffee may be passed around, the Moravian Love Feast is actually a festival that includes the singing of hymns and the playing of devotional music. The practice imitates early Christian celebrations that included prayer and sharing a meal. Moravian Love Feasts are held on holidays, anniversaries, and other special occasions.

4. B. You might see foot washing at a pre-Easter service in a Catholic church, but the Amish hold the only ceremony in which everyone gets their feet cleaned—a special adults-only communion service called Grossgemee in the spring and fall. The service lasts all day, and the adults wash each other's feet to imitate Jesus, who once washed the feet of his disciples.

5. Most likely, the Quaker. That's the only sect of the four that originated in England, and the British are avid tea drinkers. None of these groups approve of drunkenness, but all of them actually do allow moderate drinking. Amish men enjoy beer, and the others have changed their attitudes toward drinking over time. Mennonites in the United States were completely against alcohol during the 19th and early 20th centuries, for instance, but the sect has since relaxed that stance. Today, about 60 percent of Mennonites consider moderate alcohol consumption to be acceptable.